"One thing is sure.

We have to do something.

We have to do the

best we know how at the

moment…If it doesn't turn

out right, we can modify

it as we go along."

Franklin D. Roosevelt

CRY
From the Pew

A Call to Action
for The United Methodist Church

Kay Kotan

with responses by
Rodney Smothers

Market
Square
BOOKS

CRY
From the Pew
A Call to Action
for The United Methodist Church

by Kay Kotan and Rodney Smothers

©2022 Market Square Publishing, LLC

books@marketsquarebooks.com
141 N. Martinwood Dr., Knoxville TN 37923

ISBN: 978-1-950899-50-0

Printed and Bound in the United States of America
Cover Illustration & Book Design ©2021 Market Square Publishing, LLC

Editor: Sheri Carder Hood

Scripture quotations used with permission from:

CEB

MSG

NRSV

Table of Contents

Introduction

by Kay Kotan

Reformation means "a change of heart."
It does not mean "a change of head."

Napoleon Hill

If you have read any of my previous books, you likely found I come from a place of pure practicality. I often share that I never aspired to be an author. My books have come after discovering gaps in the resources needed by church leaders and from doing ministry alongside them through my consulting and coaching relationships. My motivation for writing has been as simple as this:

- There was an identified need
- I attempted to meet the need

In my work, I do not usually write about theory. Rather, I often approach writing in a systematic, easy-to-understand, action-oriented, missionally focused way while collaborating between clergy and laity along the way.

Writing this book has been much different for me than my others for multiple reasons. Having just come off an exceptionally heavy season of writing and resource creation, I had just told my publisher, Kevin Slimp, that I was done writing for a while and needed a break. Soon after I made this declaration, my husband and I left on our annual vacation to Cabo San Lucas. It had been quite an extraordinarily difficult year for us, and we both needed some genuine relaxation.

I wonder if God chuckled when I made the statement to my publisher about taking a break. As a Christ-follower, I should know better than to make such declaratory types of statements. I knew my plan, but I had not consulted with God on what God's plans might be.

During our trip, God kept nudging me that I might have something important to say. I felt God was telling me it was time to confront new challenges, mobilize my readers, and, just possibly, take my turn as a reformer. I asked the obvious questions:

- Who am I to reform the church?

- Shouldn't someone with more influence be speaking out on this topic?

- Isn't someone who already has a chair at the table better poised for this task?

- In the words of Kris Kristofferson, "Why me, Lord?"

As my resistance began to melt, the outline of this book quickly formed. I felt like God was gently nudging me for days, then walking alongside me even as I resisted. As both the outline and key points for each chapter worked their way to the page, I was reminded of the message I often share when leading consultation weekends:

> *In fact, if you don't speak up at this very important time, relief and rescue will appear for the Jews from another place, but you and your family will die. But who knows? Maybe it was for a moment like this that you came to be part of the royal family.*
>
> **Esther 4:14 (CEB)**

Perhaps it is for a moment like this that God is calling me to use my voice to offer some truth-telling and begin a conversation about the future path of our church.

I wish I could say this has been an easy task. *A Cry from the Pew* has been the most challenging resource I have written. It has been a balancing act between truth-telling, creating a sense of urgency for action, offering information and insights, and mixing in the necessary amount of compassion.

I grew up in a small United Methodist church but have spent much of my adult years in a larger suburban church. I have consulted and coached in every size church of almost every context. I have served as a contractor for conferences and districts, been employed as a lay judicatory leader, and served on two conference cabinets. I have worked as a congregational developer for church revitalization and new church starts, and I served as a jurisdictional delegate in 2016. I have extensive experience working in corporate America and have owned my own business for more than twenty years.

I have served thousands of church leaders and hundreds of congregations across the country in every jurisdiction through coaching, consulting, and speaking. I have assisted churches with revitalization, accountable leadership, simplified structure, strategic ministry planning, and visioning.

Perhaps my background has led me to such a time as this. My cry is for the church. It is a cry for direction and vision, and it is a cry to recommit to John Wesley's vision of a lay movement. I cry for adaptive leadership, and I cry for simpler, more flexible systems in the church. I cry for the space for real innovation. I cry for less bureaucracy and more accountability. I cry for the urgent need to name our current reality, reclaim our visionary roots, and recommit to the original Methodist movement, a movement that will bring clergy and laity together in mission to reach more people with the Good News.

Oh Lord, hear my cry! Oh Lord, hear the cry of your church!

This Resource

Lord, hear my prayer!
Let my cry reach you!

Psalm 102:1 (CEB)

My goal with this book is to provoke a call to action. I pray this resource will create a sense of urgency for the United Methodist Church and its members to reach new people with a new vision for the church's future.

The pandemic has disrupted our world. Do not, however, think of the pandemic as an interruption. If we act as though this time were an interruption – going back to life as it was pre-pandemic – we will miss a great opportunity.

We can't blame the current issues and concerns of the church on the pandemic. The pandemic simply accelerated what was already in motion. If we see this as an opportunity, I believe there is great possibility. The same is true for the United Methodist Church. The pandemic has created an opportunity for our denomination, and we must take advantage of the opportunity before us. I hope this resource will help kick-start conversations, offer solutions, and provoke much-needed revolutionary changes.

My intent is not to be critical of any one person or group of people. The intent is to simply name the barriers that I believe are crippling us from being the faith community Jesus intended us to be and that we can become once again. We can't address what we aren't first willing to name. My hope and prayer are that this resource will help us identify, name, and address what is holding us back. Then we can move towards genuinely creative and innovative solutions for a renewed, missionally focused, and effective movement.

Sometime – hopefully in the near future – there will be another General Conference of the United Methodist Church. How we prepare, what conversations occur, and what strategies are in place will determine the future of our church. My prayer is that this resource might be a catalyst for new conversations – including new voices – acting upon a sense of urgency, resulting in a visionary strategic plan calling us into God's preferred future for the church.

How to Use This Resource

After each chapter written by me (Kay), you will see a response by Rev. Dr. Rodney Smothers offering his perspective. We felt it essential to present different views on these various topics. Rodney's lens is through the eyes of a clergy, male, African American, East Coast, and Boomer Generation. Mine is that of a layperson, female, white, Midwestern, Generation X. I am grateful beyond words for Rodney's commitment to this important conversation.

Following Rodney's response, you will find a series of questions. In addition to personal reflection, we hope you will process these questions in a small group. We also recommend that the group set and agree upon a covenant together before beginning this journey. There may be difficult conversations, topics covered with various theological perspectives, and differing opinions along the way. Frankly, that's what Dr. Smothers and I intended. We just ask that you come to the table for conversation – led first by a disciple's heart – offering grace, listening carefully, speaking the truth in love, and desiring to find unbound pathways to make disciples who transform the world.

Gather as groups for conversation:

- Leadership groups in local churches

- District groups

- General and jurisdictional delegations

- Conference groups

- Covenant groups

- Zoom groups

- Bible study groups

- Sunday school classes

- UMM & UMW

Movements start at the fringes, not at the core, and not at the top. If we want something fresh and innovative to happen, it will need to occur organically, one person at a time, one conversation at a time, one prayer at a time until it becomes a movement with energy. With energy and with the help of the Holy Spirit, we *can* make positive changes.

We offer this resource with humble hearts and abundant

prayers, hoping others can use it to glorify God and that it can become a catalyst for the Great Commission.

CHAPTER ONE

The Cry to End Labeling

*Because of this decision we don't evaluate people by what they
have or how they look. We looked at the Messiah that way
once and got it all wrong, as you know. We certainly don't
look at him that way anymore. Now we look inside, and what
we see is that anyone united with the Messiah gets a fresh
start, is created new. The old life is gone; a new life emerges!
Look at it! All this comes from the God who settled the relationship between us and him, and then called us to settle our
relationships with each other. God put the world square with
himself through the Messiah, giving the world a fresh start
by offering forgiveness of sins. God has given us the task of
telling everyone what he is doing. We're Christ's representa-
tives. God uses us to persuade men and women to drop their
differences and enter into God's work of making things right
between them. We're speaking for Christ himself now:*

Become friends with God; he's already a friend with you.

2 Corinthians 5:16-20 (MSG)

We often use descriptors to help describe people, places,
events, objects, etc., and to help us better articulate the
picture or story. We do this to provide a more precise,
shared understanding. The intention is simple enough.
Yet sometimes those descriptors turn into permanent,
stereotyping labels, labels that are all but tattooed on our
foreheads like a flashing-light marquee. Labels can then
become divisive and drive wedges into relationships.

In the United Methodist Church, we have all sorts of labels. There is the General Conference, which encompasses the worldwide connection of United Methodist Churches. Then we label certain geographical areas (various collections of local churches) as central conferences, jurisdictions, annual conferences, episcopal areas, districts, cooperative parishes, multi-point charges, and charge conferences, to name just a few.

In addition to labeling groupings of local churches, we also have plenty of labels for the people who make up those local churches.

- bishops

- district superintendents

- conference directors

- general agency executive secretaries

- general agency directors

- jurisdictional executive directors

- elders

- deacons

- provisional members (pastors)

- licensed local pastors

- certified lay ministers

- certified lay speakers

- certified lay servants

- certified lay missionaries

- annual conference lay leaders

- district lay leaders

- local church lay leaders

- General Conference delegates (clergy and lay)

- jurisdictional delegates (clergy and lay)

- lay members to annual conference

This list covers only a fraction of the labels we use and does not even begin to include labels used in local churches, such as council/board member, nominations committee chair, to name just a few of the dozens of labels.

We have labels that refer to collections of people. Those labels include the Council of Bishops, College of Bishops, the General Conference's Connectional Table, general agency boards, annual conference cabinets, extended cabinets, and a whole slew of committees at the general, jurisdictional, annual conference, district, and local church levels. The United Methodist Church has no shortage of labels for individuals, committees, boards, areas, regions, and a plethora of other groupings.

People often introduce others – or even introduce themselves – using their labels. For example, I am so-and-so from (name your geographic setting, jurisdiction, or annual conference), and I (name your label such as pastor of such-and-such church, or bishop of a particular annual conference). We love our labels in the United Methodist Church. They are our identifiers describing who, where, and what. We use them proudly, and we use them routinely. The labels help us "place" others in their appropriate position or "box."

A problem arises, however, when people feel the need to use the word "just" when describing their role in the church:

- I am *just* a layperson.
- I am *just* a licensed local pastor.
- I am *just* a deacon.
- I am *just* a certified lay minister.

Sometimes, we're even guilty of using "justs" when describing others:

S/he is *just* a layperson.

S/he is *just* a licensed local pastor.

S/he is *just* a deacon. S/he is *just* a certified lay minister.

And no one likes it when a "just" is used to describe them. Unfortunately, both lay and clergy persons sometimes see the structure of our church as a hierarchy, where some servants are more important than others.

> *Raising the microphone, I took a deep breath, and the first words out of my mouth were, "I believe that the day of the single superstar is over."*
> **Brenda Salter McNeil**

The idea of using labels to stereotype people and groups probably never happened on purpose. Like many large institutions, as our institution has aged, it has become more sedentary and, in many ways, less flexible. After three centuries, the church has evolved into a complex institution.

Some say the church is less lay-driven and more clergy-driven than it once was, that it is more bureaucratic and less responsive. We have created more layers of decision-making and, in some ways, become less effective because of these layers.

Ethan Zuckerman warns us that we must stay engaged:

> *The danger of mistrusting institutions is that you can lose your ability to influence them.*
>
> *Deciding that you don't trust an institution can be a first step toward building new systems that work better.*
>
> **Ethan Zuckerman**[1]

Movements Have No Labels

John Wesley birthed a phenomenal movement. According to Roger Finke and Rodney Stark, sociologists and educators, the Methodist movement grew between 1776 and 1850 from 65 congregations to 13,302. This jump in congregations represented growth in the number of Methodists from 2.5 percent to 34.2 percent of the population. Finke and Stark further explain this monumental movement was attributed to "local amateur lay pastors."[2]

---

[1] https://nextbigideaclub.com/magazine/mistrust-losing-faith-institutions-provides-tools-transform-bookbite/26107/.

[2] Finke, Roger, and Rodney Stark, "How the Upstart Sects Won America: 1776-1850," *Journal for the Scientific Study of Religion,* 1989.

After 1850, however, the movement lost some traction. Finke and Stark contributed this shift to a change in expectations of clergy education and episcopal authority of local congregations:

> *The dramatic metric rise of the Methodists was short-lived. It is instructive to note that the Methodists began to slump at precisely the same time that their amateur clergy were replaced by professionals who claimed episcopal authority over their congregations.*

While the laity was turning over more responsibility to the clergy, some clergy exacerbated the situation by expressing the clergy's authority and position over the laity. In some communities, the local attorney, doctor, and clergy were the most educated citizenry. Therefore, there was an expectation that clergy "educate" their congregation since the laity did not have the same educational opportunities.

During Methodism's most rapid growth period, laity led the movement. Traveling Methodist preachers known as circuit riders (traveling Methodist preachers) rode by horseback to multiple congregations. At the time, laity not only led but were often the main preachers. Wesley was a fan and promoter of laity, as shared in his sermon entitled, "A Caution against Bigotry," in which he highlighted the importance and support of the lay preacher's ministry:

> *Beware how you attempt to hinder him [/her/the layper-son], either by your authority, or arguments, or persua-sions. Do not in anywise strive to prevent his [her] using*

*all the power which God has given him [her]. If you have
authority with him [her], do not use that authority to stop
the work of God.*

John Wesley

Wesley is also famous for this quote:

*Give me one hundred preachers who fear nothing but
sin, and desire nothing but God, and I care not a straw
whether they be clergy or laymen [women], such alone will
shake the gates of hell and set up the kingdom of heaven
upon the earth.*

John Wesley

We can once again become a movement by shedding
our labels and joining forces as laity and clergy, as
ordained and licensed local pastors, as certified lay
speakers and deacons, and as bishops and laity. Removing
the myriad of hierarchical labels, we are all simply
followers of Jesus on a mission to share the love and
grace of Jesus Christ. We are all called to the ministry
together walking the way of Jesus:

- In the same sandals

- With the same sinfulness

- As broken people serving the same Lord

- As disciples commissioned to go and make disciples

- To train and equip others in the way of the Lord, not
  in the way of the label-laden institution.

I would be remiss if I did not also acknowledge other
types of labels the church has used/is using that have/

is caused/causing pain inside and outside the church. We all know the topic around "other" labels could be a whole other book. Since this book is about the institution, I have chosen not to include these. My prayer is that by not mixing in our theological differences, more people will remain at the table to find a faithful path forward to become a transformational movement reaching new people once again for Christ.

Stereotyping Labels Have Sharp Edges

*A label locks me into a definition that
people use to control me.*

*A vision graces me with an idea
that serves to release me.*

Craig D. Lounsbrough

I have learned firsthand just how sharp the edges of labels can be when used in a way that hurts people and drives them away from the church. I relay in this chapter stories people have shared with me and examples I have personally witnessed. Others, I bear the scars left behind by the cuts of those sharp edges. We can't fix what we don't name. So, in the spirit of working toward a solution, let's name examples of the hurt and pain our label-driven institution has caused. Again, these stories and shared quotes are real-life examples.

For God shows no partiality.

Romans 2:11 (NRSV)

Label One: Licensed Local Pastor

If this church isn't going to
follow me [as an ordained elder],
you'll end up with "just"
a licensed local pastor.

I have the utmost respect for those who have attended seminary and jumped through the crazy – and sometimes ridiculous – ordination hoops to become an ordained pastor. It takes a great deal of time, money, patience, and persistence to do so. However, just because a person chose the ordination path does not make one better, more called, more effective, nor more professional than someone who chose a different path of ministry. People choose different paths based on personal decisions and circumstances.

I have worked with plenty of licensed local pastors who are incredibly effective in their ministry, sometimes more effective than some ordained elders. Likewise, I have also experienced licensed local pastors who are less effective in their ministry than ordained elders. Hence, the pathway chosen does not determine the effectiveness of ministry.

In 2020, there were 12,610 elders and 7,478 local pastors. The result is that since 1990 there are 8,352 fewer elders and 3,627 more local pastors. As elders have declined in numbers by 41 percent since 1990, local pastors have increased in numbers by 90 percent.

The Lewis Center's 2020 "Clergy Age Trends Report" [3]

---

[3] https://www.churchleadership.com/research/clergy-age-trends-in-the-united-methodist-church-1985-2020/.

*While growth was not even, there were gains in young
elders until 2016 when there were over 1,000. Then the trend
reversed. The loss in young elders since 2016 has been 261
with 80% of the losses coming since 2019. The decline since
2019 has been 24%. Just in 2021, there were 110 fewer than
in the year before. The 2021 number of young elders of 742
is not only a record low number but over 100 lower than the
previous low in 2005.[4]*

In many conferences, the number of licensed local
pastors is equal to or greater than the number of
ordained clergy. According to the Lewis Center's 2020
"Clergy Age Trends Report," licensed local pastors
outnumber elders 182 to 163 in the Tennessee Conference
and ten to zero in the Alaska Missionary Conference.
In the Northwest Texas, Iowa, Indiana, and Pen-Del
Conferences, there is an equal number of each at 113. In
conferences like Missouri, Susquehanna, West Virginia,
Kentucky, and Alabama-West Florida, the number of
licensed local pastors is growing close to equaling the
number of elders.

Yet, licensed local pastors do not have the same
voting rights at annual conferences as their ordained
elder counterparts. Ordained elders have their own
specialized gathering called the Order of Elders, and
those commissioned to start their ordination process are
recognized during ordination services. When licensed
local pastors begin their journey, their names might flash
on the screen or be printed in a bulletin at an annual

---

[4] https://www.churchleadership.com/leading-ideas/number-of-young-
united-methodist-elders-hits-historic-low/.

conference. Annual conferences hold a special service to ordain elders. Elders often process in and out of this special service in their robes and stoles. Licensed local pastors are not invited to participate. Licensed local pastors *might* get recognized on stage at their respective annual conference when they finish the course of study, likely after several years of serving a local church.

Some might say that ordained elders have sacrificed more: they put themselves at the mercy of the appointment system; they are appointed one year at a time; they make a vow to go wherever their bishop sends them. While all this is true, ordained elders are guaranteed an appointment; licensed local pastors are not. Unfortunately, fruitful, effective licensed local pastors can be tossed aside for less effective ordained elders because elders are guaranteed appointments. The process to remove an ineffective clergyperson is immensely complicated. In addition, their elder peers are the ones who make the ultimate decision for this exit.

Let's face it. Removing someone from office, especially an elder in the church, is serious business. We hope that the Board of Ordained Ministry – the group that makes ordination recommendations for the clergy to vote on – is made up of effective clergy who won't be reluctant to make tough decisions. We also hope we have an effective bishop appointing pastors to churches.

Although licensed local pastors are not guaranteed an appointment to a church, they serve one year at a time, just like ordained elders. The difference is licensed local pastors may not receive another appointment when that year is up, whereas ordained elders are guaranteed a church appointment.

Did both the ordained elder and licensed local pastor know the risks and differences when they started their ministry tracts? Absolutely. Did both understand the benefits and the disadvantages of one form of ministry versus the other? Most likely.

The stereotyping labels, however, still remain. Our system's reality is that the licensed local pastors are often removed to make room for an elder with a guaranteed appointment. Because of the different pathways chosen to serve the local church, the licensed local pastor has fewer benefits and greater risks and is sometimes seen as "less than" by their ordained elder colleagues.

Labels that stereotype positions and titles with "more than" or "less than" status have ultra-sharp edges.

Label Two: Deacons

That person is a deacon.

They can't serve [aren't called] as a lead pastor [or church planter].

Next, let's examine the label of "deacon." *The 2016 Book of Discipline of The United Methodist Church* (BOD) cites the evolving role of a deacon (¶328). It used to be that deacons used their role as a steppingstone to elder ordination, but this is no longer commonly practiced. According to the *Book of Discipline,* (¶329):

> *Deacons are persons called by God, authorized by the Church, and ordained by a bishop to a lifetime ministry of Word, Service, Compassion, and Justice to both the community and the congregation in a ministry that connects the two.*

In addition, deacons provide leadership within the church and "exemplify Christian discipleship and create opportunities for others to enter into discipleship and give leadership in the church's life" (¶329).

Some people echo the *Book of Discipline's* stated differences between the deacon and elder roles. While this distinction probably made sense at one time, the lines between the two roles have blurred in the last few decades. With fewer large churches able to afford multiple clergy and the shortage of clergy to serve churches, more and more deacons are serving as lead pastors in local congregations, but again, without the benefit of guaranteed appointments.

Some deacons chose this ministry pathway because they chose (or felt their life circumstances would not allow) not to be itinerant (move from appointment to appointment) for various reasons. At the same time, we have those ordained as elders with a guaranteed appointment who often place geographic constraints on where they are willing to serve. It seems unfair that some deacons cannot be elders because of the itinerant system, but some elders place constraints on their itinerancy.

I have had the honor of working with many deacons, some of whom have planted healthy, vital churches. Others lead existing churches with great effectiveness. This experience makes me wonder why we still limit deacons. Why are deacons often limited to serving on staff or other "supporting roles" rather than "leadership roles"? I was once told that this is not the "call of a deacon" – another example of a sharp-edged slice. In an ever-changing world, people often shift roles, positions, jobs, interests, companies, passions, etc. Even elders shift roles from leading a congregation to becoming a district superintendent, bishop, conference director, chaplain, agency/nonprofit director, and so on. Why are deacons not allowed to experience the same sort of shifts?

Permanently affixed labels cut deeply with their sharp edges as they constrain people into unfair typecasts.

Label Three: More Elders

We need to recruit more elders so we will have enough clergy eligible to serve as district superintendents.

As shared previously from the Lewis Center's 2020 "Clergy Age Trends Report," more and more persons are entering the ministry through the licensed local pastors' pathway (an increase of 90% since 1990). Yet, some believe we need to steer people toward the elder pathway because only elders can be district superintendents, and we need district superintendents to feed the church's institutional needs. As a matter of fact, on multiple occasions, I have been approached by a layperson feeling called to ministry but who was given only one possible pathway to ministry: ordained elder. They are often distraught because they have a deep sense of call, but the single pathway offered does not feel like the right fit for their life circumstances. This lack of options left them feeling that if one isn't willing to take the elder ordination route, it must mean one doesn't have a call to ministry – deep laceration!

Labels created – or perhaps evolved – to feed the bureaucracy of an institution have very sharp edges. Because of these stereotyping labels, many are overlooked or dissuaded from serving where they are called and could likely be very effective in ministry.

Label Four: Missional Strategist

There is no way a district superintendent can be a chief missional strategist for a district with so many churches.

Increasingly, conferences are consolidating, and at the same time, many conferences are moving to fewer districts. This circumstance results in district superintendents having larger geographic territories and more churches in their respective districts. Some district superintendents even have responsibility for more than one district. The financial reasons for making these moves are certainly justified and make practical sense.

However, amidst this consolidation, the 2008 General Conference added the role of missional strategist to the functions of a district superintendent (DS). The work of missional strategists is warranted and greatly needed, but it is too much to add to the long list of already-required tasks of a district superintendent.

What does it mean to be a missional strategist? By definition, a *strategist* is a specialist who develops a plan of action to carry out a particular assignment of the group. In the church world, this means a *missional strategist* is a specialist in charge of developing a plan for making disciples who transform the world.

The district superintendent's role has shifted over time from the "pastors' pastor" to a missional strategist. However, a DS spends an excessive amount of time in meetings all over their conference and beyond:

- Cabinet meetings
- Local church staff-parish relations committee meetings
- Conference committee meetings
- Meetings with pastors for evaluations, training, or consultations
- Required (or expected) training meetings as a judicatory leader
- Jurisdiction or General Conference committee and delegation meetings.

When you consider the phone calls a DS receives to troubleshoot issues, answer questions, or help problem-solve a variety of issues – in addition to all the church and charge conferences at local churches – we have some busy superintendents.

We often ask our superintendents to serve twice as many congregations due to the reduction of districts, spread out over twice the geographical area, and, let's not forget, serve in the role of missional strategist.

There is, of course, a variety of thoughts on this blended role of administration and missional strategist, as Dana Everhart offered in *The Road From Presiding Elder to Superintendent to Strategist.*[5] While some still view the role as the pastor to the pastors, others see the role as the supervisor of pastors. It is indeed an extension of the bishop's office with the authority of making appointments. Some think of this role as administrative since it is the primary connection to the paperwork that local congregations are asked to submit such as charge conference forms, annual reports, and pastor evaluations. So to add a mission strategist to the role adds an interesting twist.

I have the utmost respect for the work of district superintendents. Their job is next to impossible, in my opinion, especially now with the seemingly continuous shifts and consolidations of districts. I have many dear

---

[5] https://scholarblogs.emory.edu/candlerdmin/2017/04/21/the-road-from-presiding-elder-to-superintendent-to-strategist/.

friends and colleagues for whom I have the utmost respect who have served, or are serving, as district superintendents. Some love the role, and some can't wait to move on. Some say there are parts of the role they like and parts that do not feel like ministry at all. Most district superintendents work tirelessly. For the most part, it is a thankless, demanding job that most elders do not want or expect, but they serve at the request of the bishop.

I have often heard bishops and district superintendents speak to the "limited bench strength" in our pastoral leadership, meaning the most effective leaders are often needed to serve in our most critical areas of leadership: the local church. This situation most often translates into our most effective leaders serving in our largest, most strategic, growing churches or in a church developer's role helping multiple churches grow. Therefore, our most strategic and gifted pastors are not available to be used in district superintendent's roles. This means that often district superintendents are most gifted to serve effectively in "middle management" as administrators.

The leaders who are naturally gifted as missional strategists are often not interested in becoming district superintendents because of the administrative demands of the DS job and because their gifts are needed and critical for the local church. It is quite unusual to find a uniquely gifted person to be both a good administrator and a good strategist. The result is having a higher level of a unique leadership style being needed and called for in an archaic institutional system that piles more administrative responsibilities on leaders without the skills, experience, and likely blending of such for a single person.

Here's the problem: We are not setting these leaders up for success, and, as a result, we are compromising successful systems by forcing inadequately equipped leaders into these roles in which they must lead dozens – sometimes hundreds – of individual congregations.

When we apply labels and promote unrealistic expectations, the labels cut with super-sharp edges – pierce!

Label Five: *Just* Laity

She can't do that; she is just a layperson!

As stated earlier in this chapter, historically, the more professionalized clergy became, the more laity were disempowered, and it seems the institution promoted much of this professionalization. I sincerely believe the institution desired to provide the best, most effective clergy possible to lead and equip congregations to live out the Great Commission to build disciple-making disciples. But has it resulted in a healthy, growing church?

It can be argued that, in some ways, this professionalization has created the opposite effect. As laity became disempowered, the rapid growth of the Methodist movement began to reverse. In 1830, about five thousand preachers and laypeople left the denomination because it would not grant representation to the laity or permit the election of presiding elders.[6]

Overall, our numbers have declined every year since we became the United Methodist Church in 1968, except for a few years when larger churches grew and created a small bump of 2.53 percent in worship attendance from 1994-2000.[7]

UMC Membership	% Decline	Year	US Population	Pop Growth	% Pop UMC
10,671,774	+0.2	1970	203,211,926	13.3	5.3
9,519,407	-10.8	1980	226,545,805	11.4	4.2
8,853,455	-7.0	1990	248,709,873	9.7	3.6
8,411,503	-4.9	2000	281,421,906	8.7	3.0
7,679,850	-9.5	2010	308,745,838	9.7	2.5
6,487,300	-15.5	2019	328,239,523	6.0	1.9

http://www.gcah.org/history/united-methodist-membership-statistics, umdata.org, and https://datacommons.org/place/country/USA?utm_medium=explore&mprop=count&popt=Person&hl=en

Compare the chart above decade by decade. While the US population has been growing continuously, we see a consistent decline in membership and an ever-decreasing percentage of the population calling themselves United Methodists. In addition, the declining numbers are likely somewhat underrated since this chart shows membership

---

6   https://www.umc.org/en/content/the-churches-grow-1817-1843.

7   https://www.christiancentury.org/article/2010-09/no-shows.

rather than worship attendance. Many older churches sometimes have membership rolls that are three to five times their average worship attendance. While the average number of times a person attends worship continues to decline, most churches do not routinely clean up their membership rolls, resulting in the inclusion of deceased people and persons who moved out of the area long ago. On the flip side, newer, growing churches likely have more worship attendees than members. Regardless of how you analyze the data, there is one thing that is quite obvious: the United Methodist Church is steadily declining in both its numbers and its market share.

I suggest one of the many reasons for our decline is the disproportionate ratio of influence and authority of clergy versus laity in the church. While there is an attempt to provide equal representation in equal voting of laity and clergy at the annual conference and general conference level, the same is not true in leverage and power. The majority of positions and offices are held and led by clergy – bishop, district superintendent, conference directors, general agency general secretary, and local church pastors. While clergy make up less than one percent of United Methodists in the United States, clergy hold by far the vast majority of the decision-making influence and power within the denomination. Methodism was created as a lay movement, but it would be argued that it is now a clergy-led organization. Now laity are just laity. Ugh! If you are counting cuts, that one cuts to the bone!

In the book *IMPACT! Reclaiming the Call of Lay*

CRY FROM THE PEW

Ministry, my co-author, Blake Bradford, and I outlined multiple methods for how laity can reclaim their ministry. In the variety of settings I have been blessed to share this resource, I often challenge laity to never refer to themselves again as *just* laity. I pray our clergy colleagues will do the same.

As a clergyperson, it is easy to over-lead – and I suppose that is true in other areas of management as well. Business owners often do more than their fair share of the work because it is easier in the short term than training the staff to do the same tasks. In other words, rather than equipping laity for ministry and leadership, it is easy for clergy to over-function and over-do leadership. While some clergy are merely trying to make things easier for laypersons, some clergy over-function because they feel superior to laity instead of viewing them as less than. Whether consciously or unconsciously, clergy sometimes exhibit an air of superiority over laity rather than seeing laity as their partners in ministry. Either way, when a clergy over functions in leadership, laity are stripped of leadership opportunities.

It's my concern that the church has created a culture of clergy-centric leadership. Too often, I have attended conference level meetings in which there is no mention of laity at all. I remind them and constantly ask, "What about the laity?" We would probably all agree there are highly gifted, experienced lay people in our churches, and it is all too common we see a layperson minimized as being *just* a lay person.

I'm afraid it might sound like I'm bashing clergy, but that is not my intent at all. I have the utmost respect for clergy, their calls to ministry, and their leadership roles in the church. But too many of our clergy and laity have never been taught – or perhaps they have forgotten – that we are a denomination founded as a laity movement, served by circuit riders.

Laity are not *just* laity. Slice! Laity are, in fact, the very foundation of the Methodist movement. Once again, when we use labels to minimize, demean, and strip ownership, they slice to the bone.

Label Six: Certified Lay Minister (CLM) and Certified Lay Speaker (CLS)

> *If you decline in attendance further,*
> *you'll only get a CLM to fill your pulpit.*

Much like the earlier licensed local pastor label, the certified lay minister or certified lay speaker is often considered a lesser option to a pastor. Often a CLM or CLS is sent when a church can no longer afford a pastor. "Well, a certified lay minister or certified lay speaker is all you can afford now." This kind of statement implies that you can't afford a "real" pastor, so this is what you get. Again, we need to remember that Methodism started with laity leading congregations and providing the preaching with a circuit-riding pastor visiting the church every month or two. Today more than fifty percent of the average church budget goes to pay staff. When we were a lay-led movement, laity were happy to step up to lead and preach without expected compensation. They were living out their discipleship.

We face the danger that certified lay ministers and certified lay speakers might not always be respected for their ministry. At the same time, we have created requirements for these laypersons to obtain these "labels" (certificates) to be placed on a list for district superintendents to call when they need a person to fill a pulpit, short or long term. We have created a cumbersome process that is difficult to decipher, making it hard for conferences to implement for these certifications.

I am all for equipping people. But can't we offer practical equipping opportunities without encumbering laity in this institutional label-ism? Some of the hoops we require them to jump through are not at all helpful in their roles. There were no credentialing requirements used at the beginnings of our Methodist movement when we were equipping and deploying laity, reaching a population penetration of 34.2 percent in 1850. Currently, less than two percent of the U.S. population are United Methodists. In too many cases, we treat our certified lay ministers and certified lay speakers as second-class citizens.

Labels that promote a feeling or perception of classism are unacceptable anywhere, but we should be particularly concerned about this as the church. Once again, these labels create deep lacerations!

I assure you, servants aren't greater than their master,
nor are those who are sent greater than the one who sent them.

John 13:16 (CEB)

While the examples of labels are not an exhaustive list, it certainly provides a glimpse into the deep injuries and resulting scars of our institutional use of labels. I'm not suggesting the intent of labels is meant to injure anyone, but this is often the result. Typecasting labels divide groups, hurt people, and should have no part in the church. Each of us has a call to ministry. Suppose we are to be faithful to our call and live out the Great Commission as disciples of Jesus Christ. In that case, we need to lock arms with one another in a common charge to reach new people so that we may share the love and grace of Jesus. It's that simple.

My question appears equally simple yet seems incredibly difficult to answer: Why can't we find a way to make our system that simple?

Disruption is more than just the words we use about Jesus.
It must permeate our daily practices so that our lives
are incarnating the life of Jesus. When Jesus chose
to wash his disciples' feet, he was disrupting the assumed
hierarchy of social standing. Jesus was revealing
God's true nature to the world by taking on the form of
a servant.
Sadly, present-day Christianity is more associated
with domination and power than sacrifice and servanthood.
The most effective tools we have in discipling those
who do not share our faith are the towel and the basin.

Jon Ritner, *Positively Irritating*

CHAPTER ONE
RESPONSE
by Rodney Smothers

Kay has undoubtedly made a persuasive argument regarding the need to re-examine the labels that define lay and clergy functions. I hear her frustration with a system that is very steeped in tradition and continues to promote different classes and levels of effectiveness simply by credentialing.

Our system is broken. An increasing number of thriving congregations are led by men and women who have not gone through the traditional credentialing processes. Instead, they are leading out of a spiritual gifting that requires them to form teams of gifted leaders to assist them in succeeding in ministry. Our system is based on a credentialing process. As long as we continue to promote a system that trains and equips congregations to be run by, in many cases, "solopreneurs," we will continue to get the same results.

My mantra is, "Who will do this with me?" Kay is right: labels are limiting. There are gifted people at every level in the church who could more effectively lead through strategic seasons, primarily because their life experience, level of spiritual discipleship, and leadership temperaments are better suited for growing leaders who grow other leaders.

Kay raises the issues surrounding the role of missional strategist. This role can be redefined to intentionally evaluate the needs of local congregations so that lay and clergy resources are better assigned as teams of skilled and trained leaders with proven expertise in areas most needed in those congregations, regardless of the clergy credentialing status alone.

From episcopal offices to local congregations, new team models need to be based on changing cultural and contextual expectations of accountability and leadership, and they need to be culturally diverse, gender diverse, and theologically diverse.

One of the major obstacles to accomplishing these team models is compensation. Our current labeling structure also involves dramatically different levels of compensation. For one, since we clergy do not have lifetime appointments, we should move away from lifetime appointments for our bishops. I believe that strategic appointments across the church for specific terms would improve the results and outcomes for our episcopal leaders. Bottom line, leadership is a function, not just an office.

Questions for Conversation

1. Where have you perhaps encountered a labeling injury in the church? To the extent you are comfortable, please share the experience.

2. Share an experience where you have witnessed clergy and laity working together side-by-side with a positive Kingdom impact outcome.

3. How is your church, district, or conference intentionally bridging the gap between some of these labels, and most particularly, between laity and clergy?

4. What other organizations could we learn from to help us better understand or even model?

5. If you had the power to change anything about our United Methodist Church polity regarding labels, what would you change and why? What would be the intended outcome?

6. What are you willing to do to be a change agent for a new pathway into the future without labels? What is the first step? What partners will you recruit to help? With whom do you need an audience for conversation?

7. How can your conference support the local church's creation of more strategic team systems to equip and empower effective ministry?

CHAPTER TWO
The Cry to Remove
Layers of Bureaucracy

*God's kingdom will be taken back from you and handed
over to a people who will live out a kingdom life.*

Matthew 21:43 (MSG)

The United Methodist Church is constrained by its
bureaucracy and its *Book of Discipline*. The "Episcopal
Greetings" in the *2016 Book of Discipline for the United
Methodist Church* state the following:

> *The Discipline as the instrument for setting forth the laws,
> plan, polity, and process by which United Methodists govern
> themselves remains constant. Each General Conference
> amends, perfects, clarifies, and adds its own contribution to
> the Discipline.*

The *Discipline* defines what is expected of its laity and
clergy as they seek to be effective witnesses in the world
as a part of the whole body of Christ.

In theory, this description of the *Book of Discipline*
sounds reasonable, practical, and informative. However,
in reality, after more than two centuries of changes –
additions and deletions – the *Discipline* is encumbered with
self-contradictory language. Sometimes instructions are

incredibly vague, and at other times, filled with minute details. Among scores of other items, these details include layers of committees, boards, and general agencies at multiple levels. Examples of other details include:

- Lifetime appointments without accountability
- Processes and procedures that are complicated, time-consuming, and outdated
- Elevating people into leadership without the required skills, experiences, or gifts needed to carry out the duties of their positions effectively
- Making decisions based on compliance with polity rather than making better decisions based on current context

The system is broken. Most know it is broken and complain about it as such. However, it appears as if no one knows how to fix the broken system quickly and efficiently.

> *Bureaucracy defends the status quo long past the time when the quo has lost its status.*
>
> **Laurence J. Peter**

Like the United States government structure, the United Methodist Church comprises three branches: legislative, judicial, and executive. The legislative branch of the United Methodist Church is the General Conference, which consists of an equal number of lay and clergy delegates elected by each conference based on conference size. The number of worldwide delegates elected for the 2020 General Conference was 862 (of which 482 were U.S. delegates). The judicial branch of the United Methodist Church is the Judicial Council, made up of nine people (various splits of laity and clergy depending on the year) elected by the delegates of the General Conference for an eight-year period. The executive branch of the United Methodist Church includes all active and retired bishops who convene as the Council of Bishops and as the College of Bishops, which also includes all active and retired bishops but divides the bishops into the specific jurisdictions they serve(d).

Let's look at a few key areas causing the most dysfunction and damage to the church overall. These particular areas are not the only ones in need of a severe overhaul or elimination, but these are the ones that seem to create the most controversy and make absolutely no sense in the 21st century.

Bishop

> *Layers of bureaucracy in episcopal systems can easily smother missional effectiveness. In 1969, The Peter Principle asserted that individuals in a hierarchy tend to rise to their level of incompetence and stay there. The Peter Principle would suggest that some overseers would serve better by remaining in the parish ministry where they had once demonstrated effectiveness. However, the ecclesiastical culture is often a step worse. It is common for higher levels of denominational office to be filled with individuals who never did grow missional congregations at the local level; instead they ascended the ranks through institutional loyalty and personal connections.*
>
> **Jon Edmund Kaiser,** *Winning on Purpose*

41

The executive branch of the United Methodist Church, or the episcopacy, is quite dysfunctional. While the purpose of having three branches within an organization for checks and balances makes total sense, the three branches all still need to be functional and effective.

Let's start by taking a look at the role of the bishop. According to our *Book of Discipline* (¶403):

"The role and calling forth of the bishop is to exercise oversight and support of the Church in its mission of making disciples of Jesus Christ for the transformation of the world. The bishop leads therefore through the following disciplines:

a. A vital and renewing spirit. The role of the bishop is to faithfully practice, model, and lead the spiritual disciples of our faith.

b. An enquiring mind and a commitment to the teaching office. The role of the bishop is to continue to learn and to teach how to make disciples and lead faithful and fruitful congregations using scripture, spiritual disciplines, our Wesleyan heritage, and the history and doctrines of the Church.

c. A vision for the Church. The role of bishop is to lead the whole Church in claiming its mission of making disciples of Jesus Christ for the transformation of the world. The bishop leads by discerning, inspiring, strategizing, equipping, implementing, and evaluating the fulfillment of the mission of the church.

d. A prophetic commitment for the transformation of
the Church and the world. The bishop encourages and
models the mission of witness and service in the world.

e. A passion for the unity of the church. The role of
the bishop is to...provide leadership toward the goal
of understanding, reconciliation, and unity with
the Church – the United Methodist Church and the
church universal.

f. The ministry of administration. The role of the
bishop is to uphold the discipline and order of the
Church by consecrating, ordaining, commissioning,
supervising, and appointing persons in the ministry
to the Church and the world. The resident bishop
provides order and leads in new opportunities
for ministry within the annual conferences. The
bishop shares with other bishops the oversight of
the whole church through the Council of Bishops...
in collaboration with conference and jurisdictional
committees on episcopacy.

In ¶415, the presidential duties are outlined in
relationship to presiding in the general, jurisdictional,
central, and annual conferences. In ¶416, working with
the ordained, licensed, consecrated, and commissioned
personnel is outlined. And finally, ¶417 covers the
selection and assignment of district superintendents.

There seem to be two major flaws in our episcopacy
polity and practices. The first is the method and practice
of how bishops are elected, which, in turn, often affects
the type of leader elected to serve as bishop. The second is
the tenure of a bishop, a lifetime position.

Let me lay some informational groundwork first. Jurisdictional delegates, consisting of an equal number of lay and clergy, elect bishops. Jurisdictional delegates, again, both lay and clergy, are elected by annual conference delegates. Annual conference delegates are clergy members and laity elected by their local congregations in church/charge conferences.

There are five jurisdictions in the United States: Western, North Central, South Central, Northeast, and Southeast. Each jurisdiction comprises eight to thirteen of the 54 total U.S. annual conferences. Because some annual conferences cannot support a bishop on their own due to their membership sizes, there are currently forty-six episcopal areas serving the fifty-four annual conferences representing 30,543 U.S. congregations.[8] At the beginning of the quadrennium (2016-2020), the denomination had 66 bishops supported by the Episcopal Fund: forty-six in the U.S.thirteen in Africa, four in Europe, and three in the Philippines. According to predictions, the UMC Episcopal Fund will not support the current quadrennium's 66 active bishops across the global connection past 2023 or 2024, depending on the rate of apportionments collected.[9]

The number of active U.S. bishops has been a moving target because of delayed retirements due to the

---

[8] https://www.gcfa.org/services/data-services / and https://www.umc.org/en/content/annual-conferences.

[9] https://www.umnews.org/en/news/scrutinizing-the-proposed-hold-on-new-bishops.

postponement of the Jurisdictional Conferences and General Conference in 2020. However, beginning January 1, 2022, it appears there will be thirty-six US bishops serving after the announcement of 11 more bishops' retirement.[10]

Many active bishops are taking on expanded assignments (i.e., multiple conferences or episcopal areas) as some of the bishops who delayed their retirement are no longer able or willing to do so after a second General and Jurisdictional Conference delay. There are even a couple of retired bishops who are serving to fill in episcopal leadership gaps. At this time, no one knows how many new bishops will be elected in each jurisdiction. Election numbers will likely be dependent on the outcome of the General Conference currently scheduled for August 2022.

Now that there is a general understanding of how bishops are elected and the current landscape, it is not hard to see that the United Methodist Church is/was top-heavy. And with the average current cost for a bishop at $329,750, episcopal leadership cost is high.[11] There are way too many bishops and far too much spent on episcopal leadership, especially when the number of congregations and people attending churches continues to decline. There may be an inclination to reduce the number of episcopal leaders in the coming Jurisdictional Conferences and

---

[10] https://www.umnews.org/en/news/us-bishops-take-on-expanded-assignments.

[11] https://www.gcfa.org/media/1243/2017-2020_financial_committment_book_final_071316_02.pdf.

General Conference, but the number and how it will play out remains to be seen. With that said, however, a simple reduction of bishops is only tweaking the system. A complete overhaul is in order. More on that later.

How the election process plays out is another concern. As one who served as a jurisdictional delegate in 2016, I have seen the political dysfunction firsthand. While some jurisdictions indeed hold episcopal interviews with potential candidates, not all jurisdictions do so. Yet, we elect bishops for a lifetime. Rather than vetting bishops on their ability for "discerning, inspiring, strategizing, equipping, implementing, and evaluating the fulfillment of the mission of the church" (¶403.3), the process plays out much differently in most instances. Sometimes bishops are elected because their gender, race, or ethnicity checks a box or provides the best balance on the Council of Bishops overall. Or sometimes, they are elected due to their popularity in the jurisdiction. Perhaps the candidate is a fantastic preacher, but they haven't demonstrated their ability to plan or think strategically or evaluate their way through problems. Bishops do not have to demonstrate their fruitful practices and effectiveness to "learn and to teach how to make disciples and lead faithful and fruitful congregations" (¶403.2).

"Holy conferencing" refers to the collaborative process amongst the delegates between episcopal ballots at the Jurisdictional Conference. "Christian conferencing is a way for us to discern the will of God, to try to listen for God's voice as we are in conversation with one another," Bishop Christian Alsted points out. "Christian conferencing is about growing together in holiness. It is not about doing, it is about being."[12]

While I love the concept behind holy conferencing, I did not experience holy conferencing during the time set aside to do so. Most delegates gathered with their respective annual conference delegations to discuss their next ballot strategy, often being told how to vote by a particular person with influence and authority in their delegation. Or, a delegate from one conference would race across the room to a delegate from another conference to offer some bargaining strategy (i.e., Have your delegation vote for our candidate on this next ballot, and then our delegation will vote for your candidate on the following ballot). I can only imagine what kind of breakfast or parking lot "deals" were also in play that weekend, let alone the time leading up to the Jurisdictional Conference. Then there was the bargaining that went on at the Jurisdictional Episcopal Committee's table. This Committee decides which bishop serves which episcopal area within the jurisdiction. I am not sure what is "holy" about what I witnessed. This was politics at its best. Government elections have nothing on the United Methodist Church.

As I said, bishops are elected for a lifetime. What

---

[12] https://www.umc.org/en/content/the-5ws-and-1h-of-christian-conferencing.

other postmodern organization that is missionally effective elects or hires a person for a lifetime? If a bishop is not effective, it is nearly impossible to dismiss him/her. I often wonder if delegates voting on episcopal candidates understand that their decisions will affect church leadership and financial obligations for years – sometimes decades – to come. If a person is elected bishop without demonstrated leadership effectiveness, the United Methodist Church is committed and liable for that person for the rest of their life. At approximately $329,750 a year (salary, expenses, housing, office support) during their active years, this is a considerable number; one might even reference it as a potential liability. Bishops who take on "special assignments" to benefit the Council of Bishops can also receive additional compensation past their retirement. And, according to ¶410.2, bishops can take three months' renewal leave every quadrennium with pay. In addition, up to seven weeks of salary can be paid to a bishop between the election and effective service date.[13]

Please hear me. There are some very capable bishops, and this is fair compensation for bishops who are solid, visionary leaders. But, we do not always elect visionary, equipped leaders. In addition, bishops must often spend their time bogged down in meetings, bureaucratic processes, and administrative tasks that are meaningless and provide little to no real impact for the local church or

---

[13] https://www.gcfa.org/media/1210/2017-2020-general-conference-report-no-5-episcopal-fund-gc-approv.pdf.

its leaders, let alone real Kingdom impact.

More than once, bishops have shared their frustration with me about how their hands are tied, preventing them from providing any tangible leadership or impact, especially at the general church level. Often our most gifted elders – the only clergy eligible to become bishops – have no desire to be a bishop because they believe they can have more impact at the local church level than at the episcopal level.

Who are the bishops accountable to, and for what are they accountable? Good questions. And I wish I knew. There is an episcopal committee consisting of both laity and clergy for each annual conference. Interestingly enough, the clergy serving on this committee are under appointment of the bishop who can appoint the clergy to Timbuktu. See anything wrong there? For the most part, the episcopacy committee makes sure the bishop's residence is well-maintained and that the bishop is doing well physically, emotionally, and spiritually. Rarely are issues such as leadership effectiveness, conference goals, or vitality discussed. It is obvious why there is no such conversation given who serves on the committee.

There is also an episcopal committee for each jurisdiction consisting of two people from each annual conference (usually the first lay and first clergyperson elected) who assign bishops to their respective episcopal areas. But just like exiting ineffective elders, it is a complicated, lengthy process to exit ineffective bishops, as outlined in ¶413. Therefore, not unlike ineffective elders, conferences often ride out the time until bishops are required to retire at age 72, or they request the current bishop move to another conference and ask to receive a new bishop.

Again, what other organization runs like this? Where else could the upper echelon of leaders retain their positions when they continue to lose "market share" and membership? Yet, it feels like we are all in this tangled web that we just can't unweave. The bishops do not have actual authority to do anything different and are limited by the *Book of Discipline*. The delegates' hands are tied, bound not only by the *Book of Discipline* but by the complexities of a system seemingly impossible to change. Frankly, the local church and its leaders are confused by how complicated the whole process is and feel helpless to effect any change.

> *The bureaucracy is expanding to meet the needs*
> *of the expanding bureaucracy.*
>
> **Oscar Wilde**

Conference Leadership

Let's take a look at leadership at the conference level. Each conference has its unique structure and setup. Some conferences employ a multitude of staff, and others have very little. Sometimes this is due to conference budgets; other times, it is due to conference or episcopal priorities. And this shifts from time to time.

Some conferences have more centralized operations, while others have a more decentralized approach. The same is true for districts. Some districts have many staff persons (i.e., chaplain, two or three administrators, developer, program coordinator), while others have one part-time administrator working alongside the district superintendent. Some conferences have highly efficient processes and systems instituted, while others run on outdated and untrained staff. Although we refer to ourselves as a "connectional system," we use an assortment of technology, practices, processes, procedures, strategies, and approaches. Yes, context is crucial. However, rather than everyone inventing their own wheel, couldn't we all use the same wheel and apply our own custom hubcap? Wouldn't that be so much more effective and efficient? More on this in Chapter Four.

Furthermore, where is the strategic planning and alignment of resources to the mission and vision? If the cabinet leaders do not complete this essential work, the knowledge cannot flow down to the conference committee level. Local church committee members then act alone with limited understanding of their committee's purpose, which has likely not been explained or aligned with the overall conference mission, vision, goals, or objectives. Ironically, it is often expected that local churches complete strategic planning.

If the bishop isn't accountable for denominational growth, sustainability, or effectiveness, then who is?

District superintendents are constantly asking local churches about their vital signs (professions of faith, baptisms, people working in missions, those in discipling opportunities, etc.), but what does accountability look like for district superintendents? How about conference directors such as directors of connectional ministries, finance, church development, leadership, clergy excellence, camping, youth, etc.?

I also find it so interesting that there is often leadership development for clergy but, quite often, not for laity. Clergy are called and paid to lead the church, but they constitute less than one percent of its population. However, most funds for development are spent on that one percent. More on accountability in Chapter Four.

> *Men and women are not ordained to this*
> *ministerial priesthood in order to take*
> *priesthood away from the people*
> *but in order to nourish and*
> *sustain the priesthood of the people.*
> **Lesslie Newbigin**

I have always thought of conferences as service centers. Conferences are to be equippers and service providers to the congregations – clergy *and* laity. What if we were to believe the conference is only as strong as the weakest church? What if we prioritized the experience an unchurched person might have at any one of our churches on any given day of the week for any given reason? If the church is not a place to have this expectation, then what is? If a Christian is not expected to provide that kind of experience, then who is? Until we have higher expectations and accountability, we will continue to perpetuate mediocrity in people and experiences.

Too many organizations are over managed and under led.

Stan Robbins

More and more conferences are cutting back on services offered at the conference levels, and offices and departments are being consolidated or eliminated entirely. By and large, those leaders who do remain have fuller, unmanageable plates at best. They are often expected to lead areas with no passion or giftedness because it has been added to their existing portfolio. When churches need the most resourcing coming out of a worldwide pandemic – let alone the denominational decline and the postmodern world – many conferences lack the resources churches need and desire.

As we go into this time of General Conference, where will resources be found? As more churches close or potentially leave the United Methodist Church, more positions will likely be eliminated. How will the remaining churches and their leaders be resourced? How will the exiting process be handled efficiently, effectively, and in compliance with the *Book of Discipline* and local, state, and federal laws without sufficient, well-trained, competent staff? Will conference staff be consumed by exiting churches, leaving the churches who are staying without any resourcing at all? What kind of regrowth plan is in place, and how are we training and staffing for such? Are we creating a strategic plan for growth and vitality, or are we simply going to try to weather the storm?

> *Jean Kantambu Latting, she taught systems theory, it was a very difficult class in structural functionalism, like just a study of systems, and she used to say when systems are in place, you are either actively supporting them or actively dismantling them, there are not any neutral behaviors.*

Brene Brown's Dare to Lead Podcast
Inclusivity at Work: The Heart of Hard Conversations with Aiko Bethea[14]

Committee Complexity

The *Book of Discipline* lists page after page of recommended and required committees. Often, these committees are filled out of a sense of requirement, duty, history, or obligation rather than for strategic alignment. There are many options for simplification at the conference level, just like there are at the district and local church levels that still comply with the *Book of Discipline* (see *Mission Possible,* Third Edition, page 219 for more details). One has to get creative and go through the hard work of selling the "why" change is needed: missional alignment, accountability, better resource leverage, etc.

---

[14] https://brenebrown.com/podcast/brene-with-aiko-bethea-on-inclusivity-at-work-the-heart-of-hard-conversations/

Just like at the local church level, annual conferences have people sitting on committees for the sake of needing their names on a piece of paper. Sometimes that need for a name is dictated by the *Book of Discipline*, but sometimes it comes from the practice of a tradition that no longer has any purpose, and yet we still place people on the committee even when the *Book of Discipline* only suggests a committee rather than requires one. So much wasted time and resources in needless committees.

Conference committees should be models for local churches on how to run efficient, effective procedures and systems. Yet, in my experience, it is often the opposite. The "why" or purpose of the committee is unclear. Alignment of the mission and vision is not articulated nor expected, and accountability is primarily nonexistent. Like many local churches, conference committees are run like remote islands doing their own thing with their own agenda completely isolated from the conference.

District Superintendents

There are many gifted district superintendents and conference directors in our connection. However, because of our shortage of solid, effective leaders, bishops are often left with no other option but to appoint less-than-effective, "do-no-harm," middle-management type of leaders as district superintendents. These leaders have not necessarily grown any churches, led any movements, may lack strategic skills or vision but are steady maintainers who won't rock the boat. I get it, and I hear it so often. The leadership bench is not deep, and the strength is weak.

In light of this growing leadership crisis, an additional expectation was placed on this same group of leaders to serve as "chief missional strategist," as discussed in Chapter One. While, in theory, this is undoubtedly the direction that is needed, it seems like it is too little too late. It's as if we are trying to place Silly Putty into the hole of the *Titanic*. Not only is it too late, but we don't necessarily have the right people in place with the right tools for the job. Furthermore, districts are becoming larger in the number of churches and geographic size, so the actual bandwidth to perform this strategic work is unreasonable.

District superintendents, who make up the bishop's cabinet, spend more than half of their year absorbed in the appointive process. Most cabinets meet in December/January through May. Between meetings, there are calls and meetings with pastors and staff-parish relations chairs and committees. Depending on the conference, the DS's summer and/or fall are consumed with pastor consultations to assess how things are going and gather preliminary thoughts about the upcoming appointment season.

Mind you, some of these conversations start in July and August. So, as a pastor was just appointed – or reappointed July 1 – s/he is already being asked if s/he thinks they will be asking to stay or move nearly a year from then. For those having retirement conversations, that makes sense. But for the rest, it feels premature. For those who have been in their appointment for mere weeks, this seems just downright bizarre. Frankly, many transition decisions are made and announced way too early in the church world, causing prolonged good-byes and drawn-out transitions. The goodbye tour sometimes lasts for months and months, and I am not sure this practice is always healthy for either the clergy, staff, or the congregation.

Next, there are dual paperwork steps that are usually only a couple of months apart. The first is commonly referred to as a "clergy evaluation" held sometime around October and is completed by the local church staff-parish relations committee (SPRC). The second is the "clergy consultation," usually conducted towards the end of the year and completed by the SPRC. Often the same, or nearly the same, questions are asked on both forms. Both forms are typically sent out and received by the DS's office. Sometimes these are handled electronically, but not all conferences have the technology needed to do it this way.

Sometimes district superintendents have a second round of conversations with pastors after these forms are completed by the local church staff-parish relations committee or as a part of the routine. Besides the redundancy of the two steps (granted, one is supposed to be an evaluation, and the other is to determine appointment desires), most of the DS's time is spent in the evaluation and appointment of pastors. Again, this is essential work, but our system makes it too cumbersome, too time-consuming, and one of the most expensive staffing and recruitment systems around. Also, it makes the chief missional strategist work nearly impossible.

To layer in even more complexity, let's consider the guaranteed appointments of elders. With fewer churches, smaller churches, and guaranteed elder appointments, making appointments is quite challenging. For these reasons, there are often two, three, four, or more churches put together on a charge to make a full-time appointment for an elder. Cabinets and district superintendents do their best, but their hands are tied since they must provide appointments for elders.

Consequently, churches often pay more for compensation because they share an elder's cost with a set minimum – or more – salary, medical insurance, and pension, even though they share the cost with other churches. These forced situations usually don't work well, and new appointments have to be made often. Think of the cost to the local church, the district, and the cabinet regarding time, energy, dollars – think of moving costs alone – and, most importantly, think of Kingdom impact. Instead, churches could be appointed a part-time certified lay minister, a certified lay speaker, or a licensed local pastor with relations already established in the community – usually with much lower or no benefits as they may be bi-vocational.

When cabinets are under the restrictions of guaranteed appointments – and some conferences interpret this as guaranteed full-time appointments while others interpret it as a guaranteed appointment of any kind – there are certainly limitations to actions and implementations of a missional strategy. Instead, it turns into simply finding enough churches to fulfill the required guaranteed appointments or enough clergy to fill all the churches. Strategy and mission take the back seat – or perhaps are thrown into the trunk – to get through the process and meet the layered requirements of our self-inflicted bureaucracy.

Next comes the question of transparency. How transparent can a pastor truly be with their district superintendent? I often hear pastors comment about being careful not to get too close to other clergy because you never know who will end up being your DS. They often share this half teasingly but also know there is truth to their comment. When a DS is one's advocate at the cabinet table during appointments, a pastor must be careful how much s/he shares with their DS. Many pastors have told me they do not share too much in fear of getting a new zip code, a new "program" forced upon their church, or a detrimental note placed in the personnel file. Pastors have also often shared that they feel there is no real place to have authentic conversations within their conferences because of the vulnerable nature of the bureaucracy.

In considering efficiency and effectiveness, consider the cost of all the various district offices. Why are district offices needed? Think of the cost of the offices and the overhead to maintain them. Because of the profound number of reports and records required, there is undoubtedly a need for records storage for clergy and churches, but do we need a physical office for these records? Records can be stored digitally. And we are certainly not short of real estate for DS's to meet clergy. District superintendents and any administrative help can work remotely. We certainly proved this during the pandemic.

It would prove efficient for centralized records, standard accounting processes, and systems aligned for efficiency and effectiveness. We could eliminate a lot of expense, energy, time, paper, and wasted resources if we were to consolidate and centralize, leaving more time to focus on mission, building relationships, and resourcing leaders and congregations. This change would also eliminate districts acting like mini-conferences and align districts for the best impact and missional advancement.

General Agencies

General agencies certainly have their advantages – some more than others. However, agencies have begun to see the writing on the wall in the past decade or two. Consequently, they have begun to hunker down and aim to prove their worth. While local churches don't often understand how their apportioned dollars are being distributed, especially to our general agencies, this has become a sticking point. Even for annual conferences, it is often a mystery as to what value general agencies offer. What if local churches and conferences were part of the evaluation process and accountability for general boards and their executive leadership?

How is the effectiveness of general agencies measured? Who is measuring effectiveness, if anyone? Against what is effectiveness measured? How effectively are these agencies run? What if it were more of a pay-for-use model? Why is a seminary degree required to run an agency, but no proven experience successfully leading a large organization required? (Much like being an elder is required to be a certified coach by the General Board of Higher Education and Ministry regardless of one's coaching credentials or experience.) At this point, some agencies are being smart and innovative and moving to a self-funded model, while others are still working in the dark.

Local Churches

Like general agencies, conferences, and districts, local churches also have layers of bureaucracy and historically antiquated systems that weigh down the pathway to missional effectiveness and efficiency. Unfortunately, the leaders have been operating in this fashion for so long they don't realize there is another way to operate. They are often reluctant and mistrustful even when offered better options because it is new, uncomfortable, and "we have never done it that way before."

In working with hundreds of churches and thousands of leaders across the country, the most difficult shift to make in leadership is moving to accountable leadership. We simply are not accustomed to holding one another accountable in the church and are uncomfortable doing so, be it laity holding laity accountable, laity holding clergy accountable, or clergy holding laity accountable.

For some reason, there is this misconstrued idea that holding one another accountable is somehow not grace-filled and "isn't nice," and, as the church, we are supposed to be nice to one another. If being accountable to one another as Christians in the mission to make disciples isn't appropriate, then what is worthy of accountability? Accountability is not about punishment. Accountability means that what we are doing is important, meaningful; it is our priority and our focus. How can we be supportive and encouraging? How can we help you? What tools or resources do you need? We must work together and focus on our mission "to make disciples of Jesus Christ for the transformation of the world," as the United Methodist Church mission statement lays out. We have to get over this desire to just "play nice." It is time to move past superficial niceties. It is time to show grace and Christian love, but in the process, we may need to turn over some tables to right this ship – or perhaps we just start building a new ship.

*Jesus went straight to the Temple and threw
out everyone who had set up shop, buying
and selling. He kicked over the tables
of loan sharks and the stalls
of dove merchants. He quoted this text:*

*"My house was designated a house of prayer;
You have made it a hangout for thieves."
Now there was room for the blind and crippled to get in.
They came to Jesus and he healed them.*

Matthew 21:12-14 (MSG)

CHAPTER TWO
RESPONSE
by Rodney Smothers

The pandemic has helped us to adapt and innovate. Downsizing for the sake of downsizing is not an effective long-term strategy. Once again, I return to my mantra, "Who will do this with me?" Amazon is helping us understand the necessity of regional distribution centers. Every conference does not need its unique office of this, that, or the other. Technology is our friend. Digital, downloadable, and on-demand communication platforms exponentially increase our ability to share resources across geographical, jurisdictional, and global boundaries.

New models of shared funding by conferences, jurisdictions, and territories can create cost savings, increase team approaches, and serve as unifying factors for what will be left of the United Methodist Church in the days ahead. Our current jurisdictional models can evolve into new regional hubs that strengthen our collaborative potential and make a more significant impact through missional hubs.

While serving in the Air Force, we began our service by identifying a specific service area to be trained. The system was designed to promote skill levels, expertise, and leadership abilities, moving from basic to supervisory levels. There were – and are – compatible levels of competency and skills development for civilian employees. Post-seminary, clergy are on their own to participate in that next level of skill development. Without this intentional development, it is possible to have key leaders, district superintendents, and bishops unequipped for next-level leadership.

Perhaps we should consider special lay and clergy academies that equip and train our high-level leaders in competencies they ask others to accomplish. When Discipleship Ministries hosted the School of Congregational Development, it always struck me as strange how few of our key leaders attended that training.

We can look at several effective models in the corporate sector and realign our bureaucracy by shifting from a manager concept to a leadership concept. Ephesians 4 clearly states that our primary role is "to equip the saints for the works of ministry" (Ephesians 4:12 NRSV). Better equipped, first-level leaders equate to better results at every level beneath them. This approach would, of course, require us to unburden our bishops from administrative tasks and responsibilities that others can handle. Here is where lay and clergy teams could be of great benefit. Let us set our bishops free "to equip leaders for the work of ministry." By doing so, bishops could become more like coaches in their approach to equipping effective servant leaders.

Questions for Conversation

1. What new insights, if any, did you gain about the layers of bureaucracy in the United Methodist Church?

2. How have you experienced the bureaucracy in the United Methodist Church, and what kind of impact did it have on you?

3. What thoughts do you have about how to remove layers of bureaucracy?

4. How has your annual conference provided you and your church with resources and support?

5. How have you experienced episcopal leadership that inspired growth in personal discipleship and increased vitality in your local congregation?

6. How are episcopal and judicatory leaders held accountable for the United Methodist Church's mission, vitality, and sustainability in your area?

7. How would the role of our judicatory and episcopal leaders evolve if they assumed a coach-approach posture to equipping other leaders?

CHAPTER THREE
The Cry to Simplify

So here's what I want you to do, God helping you: Take your everyday, ordinary life – your sleeping, eating, going-to-work, and walking-around life – and place it before God as an offering. Embracing what God does for you is the best thing you can do for him. Don't become so well-adjusted to your culture that you fit into it without even thinking. Instead, fix your attention on God. You'll be changed from the inside out. Readily recognize what he wants from you, and quickly respond to it. Unlike the culture around you, always dragging you down to its level of immaturity, God brings the best out of you, develops well-formed maturity in you.

Romans 12:1-2 (MSG)

The pandemic has been a horrific time in our world history, and it will take years, if not decades, to truly discover its long-term ripple effect. We have all seen the short-term, immediate effects of this pandemic: sickness, deaths, loss of jobs, business closings, shortage of food, increase in mental health issues, disruption in manufacturing and the supply chain, and stock market instability to name just a few.

During this time, many churches launched an unplanned, multi-site ministry overnight by opening an online worship experience. Besides learning to navigate a new online presence – or handling an increased online presence – the church also had to determine how best to communicate with and care for the existing congregation. Some congregations ceased most of their ministries, while others adapted some of their ministries to online experiences. Some congregations were highly creative and delivered special ministry packets to children and older adults' doorsteps for interactive or more low-tech experiences. As Albert Einstein so brilliantly stated, "In the midst of every crisis lies an opportunity." Some churches did indeed see the opportunity and seized it. Unfortunately, other churches hunkered down and became even more inwardly focused.

Churches had to pivot, and they had to pivot quickly. The churches that had complicated decision-making structures found it most difficult to pivot and make timely decisions. Those churches that had more simplified structures were the ones who could most effectively and efficiently respond. They were more flexible, timely, and likely more missionally focused. There were no layers of bureaucracy, complexity, or confusion on who had the authority and responsibility to make what decisions.

The LORD preserves the simple;
when I was brought low, he saved me.

Psalm 116:6 (ESV)

Simplify Structure

Those familiar with the life cycle of the church know that when the structure is driving, the church is in decline. (Structure in the context of the life cycle is defined as the calendar, the facility and grounds, the budget, and how decisions are made.) Obviously, any healthy organization needs structure, but a complex or ambiguous structure can stifle or even debilitate. A healthy structure supports and helps align resources, and it should not be the driving force for all decisions or used as a power play for control or influence.

In its third expanded edition, *Mission Possible: A Simple Structure for Missional Effectiveness,* my co-author, Blake Bradford, and I have continued to evolve, share, teach, and create resources to help pastors, laity, and judicatory leaders better understand, implement, and practice both simplified *and* accountable structure. We have found that the church is exceedingly healthier when the structure is a healthy supporting actor, rather than the lead, in the life of the church especially when replaced with a leading actor of vision. It may seem a bit counterintuitive to spend time getting structure in the proper supporting role to start a new life cycle for the church, but it can happen, as I have witnessed multiple times. When structure plays the appropriate supporting role, and the leadership is willing to practice accountable leadership, the leadership board becomes appropriately missionally focused. The leadership board abandons their need and desire to manage, and often micro-manage, day-to-day operations. Instead, the leadership board invests its time in the governance lane – where most church councils spend no time – with a strategic and generative focus on stewardship and accountability.

Paragraph 247.2 in the UMC *Book of Discipline* provides the language to move to a simplified structure (referenced to as a modified organizational plan). While the language provides a general permission-giving sense for doing so if approved by the congregation's district superintendent, it is very vague in how actually to do it. While some find great joy in the vagueness, others find great distress. Frankly, this is why *Mission Possible* was initially written. Church leaders were trying to figure out how to make a "modified organizational plan" work. While some pioneers ventured out early and figured out their own plan independently, others struggled with it, and many continue to struggle.

While the concept of simplification is awesome, the implementation, especially without any direction, is difficult. Next, add the extra layer that the simplified structure still needs to comply with the *Book of Discipline*, and many find themselves lost. Bradford and I have spent more than a decade working with thousands of leaders and hundreds of churches on the ground, learning what works, what doesn't work, defining and refining, and continuously reassessing its ultimate *Book of Discipline* alignment to be able to offer *Mission*

Possible 3. It is ridiculous to expect each local church leader to make that type of investment to understand how to structure and lead a local congregation. It should be clear in the *Book of Discipline* without needing another resource to clarify. There has to be a better way.

> *Nothing stops an organization faster than*
> *people who believe that the way you worked yesterday*
> *is the best way to work tomorrow.*
>
> **Jon Madonna**

Start Over

It is hard to imagine that there is any United Methodist around that doesn't desire some sort of modification to the BOD. Of course without question, some desire more modifications than others. But, how do modifications of the *Book of Discipline* get made? According to the *Book of Discipline,* ¶501, "The General Conference has full legislative power over all matters distinctively connectional." In ¶502, it further explains that the voting membership of the General Conference consists of an equal number of clergy and lay delegates elected by annual conferences. In ¶507, the *Book of Discipline* states, "Any organization, clergy member, or lay member of The United Methodist Church may petition the General Conference." Those petitions "that have been approved by a legislative committee shall receive a vote by the plenary session at that year's General Conference," per ¶507.10. "All petitions that have been submitted to the General Conference shall receive a vote of a legislative committee," per ¶507.11.

All these steps might sound like a relatively simple process, but consider this: the General Conference in 2016 had 864 delegates speaking multiple languages – approximately nine – from across the world.

Approximately one thousand petitions were received and processed first by twelve legislative committees which make recommendations to the plenary. In other words, the petitions first have to pass through the legislative committees and be recommended to the plenary session of the General Conference for their consideration. The appropriate legislative committee has about three days to sort through the petitions and discern if the petition should be presented to the plenary of the General Conference body. Using rough averages, if there are one thousand petitions and twelve legislative committees, this means more than eighty petitions will need to be processed in a three-day period by a committee of approximately seventy people who, by and large, have no prior experience or relationship with one another, speak different languages, and are from countless cultures, backgrounds, and countries. And this is simply the first step to get the petition out of the committee into the plenary session.

Suppose the petition is recommended to be placed before the plenary of the General Conference. In that case, the petition can be modified countless times, and each modification requires speeches for and against the modification according to *Robert's Rules of Order*. Modifications and approval of new petitions can seemingly take forever, if they happen at all. Some petitions never make it out of the legislative committee. Some make it out of the legislative committee, but time runs out before it makes it onto the agenda for a plenary session of the General Conference. And yes, there are deliberate stall tactics used on the floor of the General Conference within the confines of *Robert's Rules* to delay getting to particular petitions or getting petitions passed.

Here is the bottom line: The system is broken. Very broken. The *Book of Discipline* contradicts itself repeatedly. It is too complicated. It is archaic. It takes too long to modify, especially when the General Conference only meets every four years. Rather than trying to fix it over the next hundred years, why don't we start with a new, simplified version, a version that includes the following recommendations:

- Discontinue guaranteed clergy appointments. There are so many workarounds and exceptions already in place. Elders draw demographic circles around themselves for where they are willing to serve for various reasons: an elder's spouse is unable or unwilling to relocate; a dependent of an elder needs specialized medical care in the area; the elder is needed to care for parents, grandparents, in-laws, or other loved ones and cannot relocate. Regardless of effectiveness in ministry, elders are guaranteed appointments. Their licensed local pastor colleagues may be much more effective, but because elders jumped through the additional ordination hoops, they are guaranteed an appointment regardless of their fruitfulness. The process to remove an ineffective elder is difficult, complex, and time-consuming. Let's just have an appointment system that makes appointments based on clergy effectiveness and a clergy's desired geographic area in which they are willing to serve.

• Simplify clergy exits. Once clergy are not guaranteed appointments, clergy exits will not be as critical but will still need to be addressed. An evaluation process needs to be created. When a clergy person cannot improve over a reasonable time frame with appropriate resources, their credentials to serve as a clergyperson need to be pulled.

• Discontinue lifetime bishops. Bishops are elected for a season, perhaps 6-10 years, and then retire or return to the local church to serve. There would be no such thing as once-a-bishop-always-a-bishop. Bishop elections should be conducted with more transparency, including interviewing for spiritual leadership, strategic leadership, proven leadership capabilities of growth, vitality, transformation, economic sustainability, 360 evaluations (comprehensive evaluations beyond episcopal committees including peers and others who bishops work alongside frequently such as general board secretaries, judicatory leaders, their executive administrators, conference staff, etc., raising up leaders, etc). We need a better method of discerning and selecting capable leaders who can lead us into a new direction of growth, healthiness, and vitality.

- Discontinue clergy rank. A clergyperson is a clergyperson. No rank or order. No in the club or outside-the-club, ordained or not. All clergy are valued the same, and no one has a claim over one kind of appointment or another.

- Congregational accountability. An annual conference will act on its authority and responsibility to inquire into local churches' financial, membership, and professions of faith status (¶604.8-9). When local churches are not living up to their purpose and responsibility of the Great Commission, there will be an agreed-upon corrective plan of action. If a said plan of action is not implemented, the church will no longer be chartered as a United Methodist Church. We must get over our fear of holding one another accountable. If we don't see the Great Commission as important enough for accountability, then what is important enough? More on this in Chapter Four.

- Simplify local and district structures. We need to remove all the local church, district, and conference structures as written and create a much simpler but more accountable structure that is easier to understand and creates missional alignment with greater clarity. There could be an argument to eliminate the district structure altogether.

- General agencies and general boards become separate 501(c)(3) nonprofit organizations, seek their own grant money, and create their own revenue streams.

- Complete review and analysis. In reality, the entire denomination's structure needs to be analyzed, reviewed, and considered for a complete overhaul. Is there a more efficient method by which to organize? Is the episcopal leadership model the best, or is another model better? Is the district superintendent model working, or would another model better serve local congregations, clergy, and laity more effectively? Is an appointive system still the better approach, or is it time to consider a call system where local churches interview and choose their pastors? We consider ourselves a connectional church, but are we? Is this something that is still highly valued? How can the denominational layers be simplified, leaving more resources for Kingdom impact at the local church level?

As Shandon Klein asked, "Do we need the institution to do church?" In her insightful article, Klein explains that discipleship is at the core of what sets the church apart from other institutions:

> *Without making disciples that follow the way of Jesus Christ, we are just another institution, stuck in its own ideological bunker, living for itself instead of its creator.*

> *With that said, as the United Methodist Church stares in the face of the opportunity to restructure and refocus as a "church," we must take a look at the mirror, examine our fruits, and ask the hard questions....The choice is ours: are we a "church" first? Or an "institution"?*[15]

---

[15] https://www.umc.org/en/content/do-we-need-the-institution-to-do-church.

Practical Simplicity

While we are working on the topic of simplicity, let's cover a few concepts on simplifying churches in general.

First, we need to help people understand the distinction between *mission* and *methods*. So often, we get mired down in our methods, mistaking them for something more. If we aren't careful, our methods become the mission, and we adhere to them as if they are somehow sacred. A method, however, is **how** we achieve a desired outcome. Once implemented, though, if a method does not work or the situation changes, that method will need to be changed. For example, just because one bridge is out doesn't mean we can't get to the other side of the river. It simply means we must find another way to get there. Maybe we need a new bridge or a new route, but we don't give up getting to the other side altogether.

Another way to think about the same concept is to consider your church's ministries. Ministries are the methods. The ministries are **how** churches carry out the mission of making disciples and in which a church helps congregants grow in their discipleship or take their next faithful steps. While the need for discipleship remains constant, the different steps to get there (the **how**) change over time. For example, the confirmation class in 2021 did not have the same experiences as the confirmation class in 1972. We can't get stuck in our methods.

Secondly, church members often become attached to the church building. When people refer to "the church," they are more often than not referring to the facility, not the body of Christ. We have reached the point where our church identities are intricately entangled in our buildings for various reasons:

- People have often experienced big life moments inside the church building, such as weddings, baptisms, funerals, and confirmations.
- Memorials for a loved one are commemorated inside the church building, such as a beautiful stained glass window, a donation towards the organ, or a piece of artwork with a gold plaque engraved with the name of a loved one.
- Inside the church is where some have felt closest to God because of meaningful worship experiences over the years.
- The building signifies those big life moments, remembrance of our loved ones, and our God moments.

Often churches spend the majority of their resources – time, energy, and money – caring for their buildings, leaving little to nothing left for the mission of reaching new people. In their book *Fresh Expressions of People Over Property,* Audrey Warren and Kenneth H. Carter, Jr., recall how John Wesley, founder of the Methodist movement in England, is appreciated for adapting even factories into sanctuaries as a place to preach the gospel. Wesley spoke boldly about Methodist preaching houses, which should be different from sanctuaries or cathedrals. Wesley said:

Let all preaching houses be built plain and decent,
but not more expensively than is absolutely
avoidable. Otherwise the necessity of
raising money will make rich men necessary to us.
But if so, we must be dependent upon them, yea,
and governed by them. And then farewell to
the Methodist discipline, if not doctrine, too.

When property is valued more than people, we
miss the love that binds us together and our
assets shift from promise to problem. Churches
that act in faith to take a property to let God
make a promise will be those that see a future.

We all know the church is not the building, right? So why do we as congregations spend so much time, money, energy, and resources on our buildings? Think how much more we could do for the Kingdom if we didn't invest as much – or perhaps anything – in buildings.

The pandemic has highlighted the third concept for more simplicity. Many companies learned their employees were more productive and often happier working remotely. The overhead was less for the companies, and the employees felt they had more flexibility, wasted no time commuting, and were more accessible to their families.

Many United Methodist district and conference offices also closed during the pandemic but have since re-opened. And, even with so many conferences consolidating districts, they are still maintaining district offices. Why? There is plenty of real estate owned by local churches that could be used for district or clergy gatherings if needed. District superintendents and their support staff worked remotely during the pandemic, so why couldn't they continue to do so? We live in the 21st century. All records should be digital, so there is no need for an office to accommodate files. District superintendents spend most of their time on the road, in cabinet meetings, or meetings at churches. There is no need for the expenses of a district office. The same is true for conference offices. If we consolidated administration for all districts into one service center, the church could save so much in real estate, utilities, and human resources expenses.

The proverbs of Solomon, King David's son, from Israel:
Their purpose is to teach wisdom and discipline,
to help one understand wise sayings.
They provide insightful instruction,
which is righteous, just, and full of integrity.
They make the naive mature,
the young knowledgeable and discreet.
The wise hear them and grow in wisdom;
those with understanding gain guidance.
They help one understand proverbs and difficult sayings,
the words of the wise, and their puzzles.
Wisdom begins with the fear of the Lord,
but fools despise wisdom and instruction.

Proverbs 1:1-7 (CEB)

CHAPTER THREE
RESPONSE
by Rodney Smothers

I don't disagree with Kay's suggestions for improving how we are structured at the general and local church levels. I would bring to the forefront that any changes that we propose must be sensitive to the unaddressed impact on churches that operate with different cultural dynamics.

In Kay and Blake Bradford's resource, *Mission Possible: A Simple Structure for Missional Effectiveness,* there is intentionality regarding the need to discern how spiritually shapes emerging leadership structures. Their observation that "accountable leadership is about moving away from making decisions based on people's personal preferences" alone is moving the conversation in the right direction. I advocate that a greater sensitivity to cultural, racial, and contextual impact needs to be included in the conversation.

Some of the new ministries that will emerge will be multi-cultural. My experience has taught me that the majority of cultural experiences often set up expectations based on the past that often inhibit a smooth transition when changing leadership structures. This sensitivity should be intentionally addressed in any discussion regarding change. Hear these comments, not as disagreement rather as an invitation.

Race, gender, theology, and culture are fibers that run through all leadership settings. Without sensitivity to who is or is not sitting at the table when shaping thoughts and conclusions, we run the risk of doing a disservice to the transformational process. While Kay does advocate "bringing different voices, experiences, and expertise to the table," what I am not as clear about is that when she makes a powerful case for deploying more people for ministry and involving fewer people in administration, that she has fully considered that in smaller congregations and congregations of color, the available bodies for administration and ministry are too few to separate.

The economic, political, and social dynamics in this present age compel me to press for a deeper discussion regarding inclusivity, equality, and justice. Simplifying our structures is necessary, but not at the cost of unintentionally disenfranchising anyone. I don't hear Kay's intent to disenfranchise anyone. My intent is to add additional perspective to the discussion so that no voices are lost in this conversation.

Questions for Conversation

1. How would you describe simplified structure? In your experience, does the United Methodist Church fit your definition of simplified structure? Why or why not?

2. Provide one or two examples of how you might suggest simplifying the local church. Share with your group.

3. Provide one or two examples of how you might suggest simplifying the district or conference. Share with your group

4. Has your local congregation ever experienced confusion between *method* and *mission*? If so, share the story and how it was resolved or how you could have seen it resolved in retrospect.

5. Where would you rate your congregation on its value of mission versus facility? What percentage of your budget is spent on building and maintenance? How much time is spent at church council meetings discussing building and grounds issues versus the making and maturing of disciples?

6. If you could simplify one thing about the *Book of Discipline*, what would it be and why?

7. What considerations of inclusivity, equality, and justice have been neglected at your local church level for the sake of simplicity or ease? The district level? Your annual conference level?

CHAPTER FOUR
The Cry for Accountable Leadership

It has been my honor and privilege to coach clergy from all over the country for over a decade. These clergy include a combination of highly seasoned and newly ordained ministers, second-career licensed local pastors, deacons, elders, certified lay ministers, commissioned, and everything in between. This collection of leaders has also included church planters, planting teams, district superintendents, church developers, pastors leading church revitalization efforts, judicatory leaders, conference lay leaders, local church council chairs, district lay leaders, conference staff, and many other dedicated church leaders.

Through these thousands of hours of coaching, there is one theme that comes up continuously from or in relation to seminary-trained clergy: "I was not at all trained to lead this (situation, church, circumstance). I was trained to preach and teach, but not how to lead."

Interestingly enough, I was at a gathering of judicatory leaders assembled by a seminary dean to gain insights and feedback. The question was asked about how well their graduating seminary students were equipped for serving the local church. At first, the judicatory leaders were wondering if the seminary dean really wanted the feedback requested. A softball kind of response was offered initially, but the frustrated judicatory leaders opened up before long. The gap in leadership skills of seminary graduates was cited over and over with specific examples.

The dean grew increasingly agitated and abruptly stopped the conversation. Surely we judicatory leaders had misunderstood the question. The dean then explained that the seminary's responsibility is to form theologians, and it is the annual conference's responsibility to form leaders. Ding! Ding! Ding! There's the disconnect. This seminary did not see leadership development as its responsibility, but the conference expects seminary graduates to have leadership skills.

It is quite possible to have a seminary graduate with a bachelor's degree and an M.Div. with little to no leadership development or experience. Yet, they are often sent to a small church or multi-point charge in the middle of nowhere and are expected to learn on the job where leadership is not always well practiced or modeled. Worse yet, these pastors often learn bad habits on how a church runs and are at an extreme disadvantage when they get to a larger church. Once the training ground for young clergy, fewer and fewer larger churches can afford to take on associate pastors. Sometimes a seminary student can find a summer job or internship at a church, but it is likely taking children/youth to camp or cleaning out the resource room. We often miss the opportunity to pour into young clergy these vital leadership skills. We place them in positions we can't get anyone else to take instead of viewing this as an investment in the future of a clergyperson that will pay dividends for decades to come.

Consider the situation we have placed young clergy persons in today. They will likely graduate with a mountain of student debt and start their first full-time job with a master's degree at $40,000. In addition, it will take an additional three to five years for them to finish the process to be ordained into the "system." It is no wonder why fewer and fewer younger adults take the pathway to become a United Methodist ordained clergy. The pathway is lengthy, expensive, and the denomination is shrinking. What kind of future is that?

As referenced in Chapter One, while the hoops for the professionalization (i.e., ordination) of clergy have increased in size and number, the role of laity has continuously diminished. It is interesting to note that in one of Wesley's sermons titled "A Caution Against Bigotry," he states:

> *Beware how you attempt to hinder him [layperson], either by your authority, or arguments, or persuasion. Do not in anywise strive to prevent his using all the power which God has given him. If you have authority with him, do not use that authority to stop the work of God.*

John Wesley

So, we find the denomination in this interesting conundrum. We have clergy required to go through an ever more complex, time-consuming, expensive process to get into the ministry, and we have ill-equipped laity who have been shut out of leading and doing ministry, all while the denomination is in a nosedive of decline. As Dr. Phil would say, "And how's that working for you?"

Do we not see the connection in all of this? Increased professionalization of clergy is not working. In fact, it is counterproductive. In addition, the increased professionalization is, by and large, not even equipping clergy to be leaders, a required trait to be a local church pastor. Add to that the fact that leadership development is being removed from conference staff and budgets in their ongoing shrinkage.

Clergy morale overall is not good. While weariness was the theme I heard from clergy in 2020, just plain worn out and wondering about next steps was the theme in 2021. Leaders have had to navigate a pandemic that obviously no one was prepared or trained for which only perpetuated and magnified any issues already ailing local churches. Some of our older clergy leaders are considering retiring earlier than planned. Some of our younger clergy are seriously considering alternative career pathways.

Numerous clergy under the age of forty have shared with me that they can no longer imagine staying with the church for their entire professional career. They are doing what they have to now so that they can have alternative options in the next couple of years. Now there is alarming data to support what I have been hearing in my clergy coaching sessions.

In an October 2021 Barna study with pastors' well-being on the line, and many on the brink of burnout, 38 percent indicate they have considered quitting full-time ministry within the past year. This percentage is up 9 full points (from 29%) since Barna asked church leaders this same question at the beginning of 2021.

One of the more alarming findings is that 46 percent of pastors under the age of 45 say they are considering quitting full-time ministry, compared to 34 percent of pastors 45 and older. Keeping the right younger leaders encouraged and in their ministry roles will be crucial to the next decade of congregational vitality in the U.S.

Another notable gap emerges based on denomination, with pastors from mainline denominations far more likely to consider quitting than those from non-mainline denominations (51% vs. 34%). Other significant differences arise among gender, with female pastors being far more likely than male pastors to have considered giving up full-time ministry, and ministry tenure. This same study also noted that only one in three pastors is considered "healthy" in terms of well-being.[16]

---

[16] https://www.barna.com/research/pastors-well-being.

Apathy

In a community, people are held accountable for negative attitudes that would give rise to apathy.

A failure in community creates conflict. A failure in leadership creates apathy.

Your organizational community is relationship driven.

Your organizational culture is leadership driven.

Doug Dickerson[17]

Over the past few years, I have noticed a growing sense of what I refer to as congregational apathy. The symptoms are identified as a desire and openness for great things to happen, but no energy, personal commitment, or tolerance for any needed changes, or sense of urgency for the great things to come to fruition. Commonly – and especially in declining, aging congregations – there is the thought that if only a few young families would walk in the door and become instantly involved, magically, all would be well again.

A standard definition of *apathy* is a lack of emotion, feeling, interest, indifference, lack of involvement, or a non caring attitude. Often the term *apathy* is used to describe a person; however, communities, organizations, and institutions can also have a culture of apathy. According to Athina Benik of AskingLot.com, "An apathetic culture shows minimal concern for either people or performance. A caring culture exhibits

---

[17] https://www.dougdickerson.net/2019/05/12/how-to-defeat-a-culture-of-apathy.

high concern for people but minimal concern for performance issues."

What does all of this mean? Each congregation is unique. It is set in a unique community, has a unique history, unique congregational gifts, unique mission field needs, etc. Yet, each church is called to the same mission: to share the Good News of Jesus Christ and carry out Jesus' command to make disciple-making disciples.

As mainline protestant churches, we have all drunk the same proverbial Kool-Aid and fallen into some of the same institutional potholes. We have become far too pastor-centric. When a congregation expects a pastor to provide the vision and make most of the decisions – and the pastor does so – the congregation has little ownership of those decisions or vision. We have also become far too staff-driven. When a congregation hires staff as ministry "doers" rather than equippers, the congregation becomes too dependent on staff doing the ministry on behalf of the congregation.

We have also become dependent on attraction for growth. Some congregations rely on fancy buildings, high-tech investments, or alluring programming to "attract" new people rather than learning how to share their faith stories and invite people to follow Jesus. These now-all-but-dead attractional models have failed to bring new people into the life of the church.

Because of these three primary shifts (pastor-centric, staff-driven, attractional-dependent growth), we have strayed from our core purpose of discipleship. Without discipleship as our primary driver over the past several decades, 70 to 80 percent of churches are in decline. This overwhelming decline and the side effects caused by the three shifts have led to congregational apathy. Those shifts' side effects have resulted in the following:

- Congregations focus more on caring for one another, leaving community care for others

- Less involvement from parishioners since the staff is doing the ministry

- Less interest and passion since the pastor is casting the vision and making the decisions for the entire congregation.

These are all indicators of apathy. Add to this the lack of accountability that Dickerson points out, and there is no way around an overwhelming upheaval of apathy.

Where is the hope? Since apathy is often described as the loss of motivation manifesting as a reduction of goal-directed behavior, congregational apathy can sometimes be reversed with a renewed missional focus. Missional focus starts with congregational visioning, discipling, leadership development, and strategic ministry planning. The key is not waiting until it is too late for congregations. The same is true for our institution.

Accountability

To even mention accountability in the church is often met with instant push-back. Somehow, the idea that accountability is "not nice" or "grace-filled" has become commonplace among clergy and laity leaders. For some reason, accountability has primarily negative connotations in the life of the church and is widely misunderstood; it is deemed as punitive or punishment. Accountability, however, is such a powerful leadership tool that can be empowering, motivating, and collaborative. Since accountability is such a vital partner of simplified structure, Blake Bradford and I commissioned a video to demonstrate the practice of accountability during a leadership board meeting. You can find that video at *kaykotan.com/sas/*. Many have found the video to be a helpful tool for demonstrating a deeper understanding of accountability and how it can bless a church when practiced well.

> *Requiring accountability while also extending your compassion is not the easiest course of action, but it is the most humane and ultimately the safest for the community.*
>
> *Vulnerability is the source of hope, empathy, accountability, and authenticity.*
>
> **Brené Brown**

For accountability to truly work, be trusted, and be implemented well, it must be practiced at all levels. Yet, our denominational institution lacks trust overall. At the very time when people are seeking purpose, meaning, and community with greater intentionality and desire, the church seems to be in its least likely state to offer any of those three. In a New York Times article, Yuval Levin explains why this is the case:

> But what we are missing is not simply greater connectedness but a structure of social life: a way to give shape, purpose, concrete meaning and identity to the things we do together. If American life is a big open space, it is not a space filled with individuals. It is a space filled with these structures of social life – with institutions. And if we are too often failing to foster belonging, legitimacy and trust, what we are confronting is a failure of institutions. This social crisis has followed upon a collapse of our confidence in institutions.[18]

It is interesting to see how the need for a sense of belonging, purpose, and impact, desire for authenticity, transparency, and vulnerability, the meaning of the things we do together, and the lack of trust in institutions are all tied to the failure of institutions.

Over the past few years, the United Methodist Church has not given the public, let alone our leaders and congregations, much alternative information about our own institutional failure with headlines such as these:

- **Mt. Bethel files complaints against UMC bishop, district superintendent,** *Atlanta Journal-Constitution,* April 27, 2021

---

[18] https://www.nytimes.com/2020/01/18/opinion/sunday/institutions-trust.html.

- **Texas Megachurch Pastor Sent to Prison for Fraud Scheme**, *NBC DFW*, January 15, 2021

- **Historic Houston church leaves United Methodist Church over LGBTQ stance**, *Religion News Service*, April 29, 2021

- **Conservative United Methodists Plan Breakaway Denomination**, *Christianity Today*, March 2, 2021

- **Why the split in the Methodist Church should set off alarm bells for Americans**, Washington Post, January 16, 2020

- **Churches across theological spectrum exiting**, *United Methodist News*, April 19, 2021

- **Illinois megachurch leaves UMC amid LGBT debate, retains ownership of campuses**, *Christian Post*, May 21, 2021

- **UMC Pastor Loses License for Marrying Same-Sex Couple in Tennessee**, Christian Post, March 6, 2018

- **Former O.C. pastor gets 15 years to life in prison for molesting 7 girls**, *Orange County Register*, February 9, 2021

- **8 bishops join in planning new denomination**, *United Methodist News*, March 12, 2020

- **Confirmed: Voter Fraud at General Conference 2019**, *Insights*, August 22, 2019

While the world looks on, this is what they see: a denomination in chaos. And it is further proven in recent research. In a 2021 Barna Cities Initiatives Study, 80 percent of practicing Christians have a favorable view of the church, while only 21 percent of non-Christians think of the church in a positive way. How will we ever come out of this and be able to build trust? Where is the accountability for the decline and continued chaos? The system is broken. How can we fix it?

The very people with the most authority feel their hands are tied to make any real change. Our bishops have influence but no vote. And on more than one occasion, when the bishops made a decision, they almost immediately decided to reverse the decision. For example, take the decision for a virtual, special-called General Conference session in 2021. On February 25, 2021, it was announced that there would be a special session on May 8, 2021, only for it to be canceled on March 22, 2021. Or, how about the uncertainty on whether or not bishops are going to retire? Some bishops were going to retire, then they weren't, and then suddenly they will retire. Is there a recommendation or not to elect bishops in 2022? Which is it? We are all in uncharted territory. If ever we need leadership to step up and lead, it is now. Having our episcopal leadership so seemingly indecisive is unsettling at best, creating concerns of delegates regarding bishops' overstepping their authority as reported.[19]

Let's not forget about local church accountability.

---

[19] https://www.umnews.org/en/news/scrutinizing-the-proposed-hold-on-new-bishops.

The *Book of Discipline* ¶604.8-9 unequivocally shows the intent to hold congregations accountable for their fruitfulness: "an annual conference will act on its power [one might even argue responsibility] to inquire into the financial, membership, and professions of faith status of local churches."

Yet, what annual conferences actually do this? I have often been told that if the cabinet of an annual conference were to actually hold a church accountable for no professions of faith, all churches would revolt against the annual conference for "picking" on a small church. Again, I grew up in a small United Methodist church, and I have nothing against a small church. There are healthy, vital small churches. However, I believe all churches are responsible for the purpose for which they were formed and that responsibility continues for as long as they are in existence. If they no longer serve that purpose, why do they still exist?

> *Venerable structures, whose usefulness has long since calcified into crippling rigidity, make it hard for winning innovations to emerge. Some episcopal denominations are blessed and cursed with ostensible lifetime appointments for their clergy. This apparent guarantee does not easily lend itself to serious accountability. It's a good thing that none of the original churches addressed in the New Testament have survived to the present day. Can you imagine a 2000-year-old congregation that says, "We've never done it that way before?"*
>
> **John Edmund Kaiser,** *Winning on Purpose*

While the guaranteed appointment of the ordained elder and the lifetime election of bishops has been addressed previously, it seems appropriate to remind us of this polity under the topic of accountability. Guaranteed appointments simply do not coincide well with accountability. A guarantee is a formal promise or assurance, and it is not conditional. The initial requirements were fulfilled, but no ongoing, stated requirements are easily measured and evaluated with clear and expeditious exit strategies. Therefore, there is no actual ongoing accountability.

What the Church Can Learn from a Franchise Business Model

There is sure to be backlash for this next point, but it is worth the risk for some who might be open to consider the lessons we can learn from the comparison. What could the franchise business model teach us about denominational churches? While I am not suggesting a franchise model for churches, some lessons and principles could be helpful as we consider a healthier, more vital future for our faith communities.

In a franchise model, someone has already developed a business model. That model has been tested, tweaked, and proven in multiple settings. Processes and procedures have been created. Manuals have been written. It is a proven, profitable business. For someone desiring to start a new business, there is a significantly lower failure rate investing in a franchise business than starting one's own business from scratch. You not only have a proven business model, but you have a person or company to walk alongside you as you start and grow your business. Rather than having to make the mistakes and learn from them – and likely also pay for them in time, frustration, and dollars – the franchise has already made them and can prevent you from making those same mistakes. To some degree, this is what I think the original intention of the connectional church was supposed to be all about. We share resources and systems. We learn from one another.

Here is a great example. In the *Church Outreach Assessment,*[20] 70 percent of church leaders, in their view, do not have an effective process for assimilating first-time guests. Thirty-five percent say they have no process, and the remaining 34 percent say the process they have is not effective. Just like knowing how to create and implement a discipleship pathway, wouldn't an assimilation system be a basic tool pastors should be taught in seminary or course of study? I can assure you that this type of basic process would not only be taught in a franchise model, but there would be a step-by-step process documented in a manual that anyone could pick up and implement.

Here is something else we can learn from the franchise model. There are consequences when a franchise

---

[20] https://careynieuwhof.com/church-outreach-assessment/

location does not follow franchise protocols, branding requirements, procedures, pay their franchise fees, or have poor customer service evaluations. First, there is help dispatched to try to correct the situation. And, this help is dispatched very quickly. They don't mess around with substandard practices or outcomes. It is in everyone's best interests for there to be a turnaround. But, if the situation is not corrected in a reasonable time frame, the franchisee will lose their franchise, and the location will be closed, or another franchisee will take over. The franchise will not jeopardize its brand.

Franchisers realize that if too many customers encounter a location with a bad experience to their brand's expectations, they will lose market share beyond just that particular market. The franchiser understands the greater impact and the ripple effect that one location can have on other locations and, ultimately, the brand overall. Either we, the church, don't understand this, or we have chosen not to do anything about it. Why is this the case? The *Book of Discipline* gives the authority and expectation for accountability (¶604.8-9), but conferences, by and large, have taken no action and no responsibility.

Servants, do what you're told by your earthly masters. And don't just do the minimum that will get you by. Do your best. Work from the heart for your real Master, for God, confident that you'll get paid in full when you come into your inheritance. Keep in mind always that the ultimate Master you're serving is Christ. The sullen servant who does shoddy work will be held responsible. Being a follower of Jesus doesn't cover up bad work.

Colossians 22-25 (MSG)

Leadership Development

There is a lack of leadership development at all levels. More often than not, our lack of leadership development has created pastor-centric congregations with ill-equipped leaders. We have come to our day of reckoning when it is time to admit that we have an outdated institution where most of our church leaders (clergy and laity) do not lead and do not know how to create a movement of disciple-making disciples. The church used to be the place where leaders were developed and deployed into the community. But now, the church often depends on the secular and corporate world to do this leadership development work.

Only in the past decade or so have some conferences invested in any leadership development, and most of that has focused solely on clergy. Again, there is a glaring oversight that conferences do not also focus on laity leadership development, 99 percent of the United Methodist Church's composition. Most leadership development is for clergy. Now, I am not referencing the often-ridiculous hoops required for a layperson to become a certified lay minister or a certified lay speaker as specified in the *Book of Discipline*. I am only speaking of *leadership* development.

Even something as basic as leadership development in the local church is missing. Most churches do not realize that the nominations committee is actually called the "committee on nominations and leadership development" and that this committee is responsible for leadership development for the congregation. Although often practiced in this manner, this committee is not about figuring out who we can arm wrestle into saying yes to allowing the committee to place her/his name on a piece of paper that the district office requires for some fall meeting. Again, laity have been stripped of their opportunity to be equipped to lead. For the most part, we have laity that don't know what they don't know. They have not been adequately trained and have not been provided the proper tools for ministry.

The pastor is the chair of the Committee on Nominations and Leadership Development. Does this mean the pastor is unaware of this committee's responsibilities beyond getting people to serve on the committees? Have the pastors not been trained and equipped? In my experience, pastors are at a loss as to how to create a leadership development process. And, so, the issue perpetuates itself.

For the church to be vital in decades to come, we must invest in the future *now*. This means we need to invest in future leaders *NOW*. This means we must create a culture of innovation and experimentation. This means we must be willing to be adaptive and flexible. There will undoubtedly be a huge learning curve for churches and their leaders, and that is okay. In my experience, our current culture, *Book of Discipline*, and practices box us into tradition, the "tried and true," and "the way we've always done things." In fact, the system actually drives out innovative leaders, people who ask questions, and those who seek more efficient, effective means to accomplish fruitful ministry. Vital organizations have a budget for leadership development and research and development. Yet, this is the first thing that our denomination cuts. We won't survive, let alone thrive, if we continue to have this kind of short-sighted view of the future. Maybe we don't have our sights on the future. Perhaps we are simply in survival mode.

Our denomination talks a big game about the importance of being a lifetime learner. Yes, this is a good thing. But being a learner without being an implementer is a waste. We must create and value a culture of innovative leaders. We must value and reward these kinds of people, too. Too often, these are the people that we don't know how to work with or direct. So then we often underutilize them or put them in situations where they are frustrated, undervalued, or not supported. Therefore, we often end up losing them to another organization who has a culture which cultivates this type of innovative leader. We have not created a culture that supports and nurtures the people we need to build a vital, healthy organization for the future.

It is important to note that adapters are people who change because they are forced to change due to current circumstances or people. Innovators change voluntarily. They have a desire and are self-motivated. Adapters are not seeking change; they come along because they have no choice. Therefore, adapters may retreat to the way things were once the circumstances causing the change are no longer present. Innovators tire of the status quo and less-than-stellar outcomes. Adapters have to be dragged along. Innovators are self-starters.

> *He gave some apostles, some prophets, some evangelists, and some pastors and teachers. His purpose was to equip God's people for the work of serving and building up the body of Christ until we all reach the unity of faith and knowledge of God's Son. God's goal is for us to become mature adults – to be fully grown, measured by the standard of the fullness of Christ. As a result, we aren't supposed to be infants any longer who can be tossed and blown around by every wind that comes from teaching with deceitful scheming and the tricks people play to deliberately mislead others. Instead, by speaking the truth with love, let's grow in every way into Christ, who is the head. The whole body grows from him, as it is joined and held together by all the supporting ligaments. The body makes itself grow in that it builds itself up with love as each one does its part.*
>
> **Ephesians 4:11-16 (CEB)**

The United Methodist Church has evolved to house and nurture the shepherds and teachers. However, the United Methodist Church institution is no longer equipped nor structured to handle apostles, prophets, or evangelists. Apostles, prophets, and evangelists do not fit well in the United Methodist Church "institutional box" Therefore, the United Methodist Church does not reflect the whole body of Christ. Thus, the body is not healthy and is unable to function properly to its fullest potential.

The institution has alienated the apostles, prophets, and evangelists with its *Book of Discipline*, polity, practices, inability to adapt, lack of accountability, and spending so much time and energy in conflict.

> *No major denomination in the United States regards apostolic ministry to card-carrying, secular, pre-Christian outsiders as its priority or even as normal ministry.*

George Hunter III

CHAPTER FOUR
RESPONSE
by Rodney Smothers

Kay's discussion regarding the seminary's role in creating – or failing to create – strong leadership models is interesting. Having served on seminary faculties as an adjunct, I have had my feet in both worlds as a professor and practitioner. In the world that I serve in today as a pastor and leadership coach, I hear the discussion regarding the failure of seminaries to prepare pastors for ministry but jump to what I think is a larger failure in our system. A Master of Divinity should not be thought of as a terminal degree for the pastor or laity track.

Lifelong learning and certification should continue throughout a person's season of service. Cohorts, coaching, consultations, collaboration, and counseling are lifelong disciplines. Currently, we train pastors to become "solopreneurs." That model is obsolete. We should have laity and clergy in certification processes, side by side, modeling the team approach to ministry. The most important question that laity and clergy can ask of one another is, "Who will do this with me?"

We also need to supplement our seminary education with other disciplines found in the workforce to graduate from seminary with a normal inclination to work in collaborative partnerships. Highly motivated lay and clergy leaders pay large sums of money to be coached, attend seminars, and obtain post-seminary certifications just to stay current. These training opportunities should be included in conference budgets to produce next-level lay and clergy leaders for long and fruitful service.

The harm being done to our post-pandemic lay and clergy leaders because of an inadequate denominational response is criminal. On the other side of the General Conference, we will have saved a few buildings but lost a valuable workforce of leaders because we have not invested in innovative, transformational, and resilient leaders.

Regardless of what the General Conference decides, the urgent leadership need is retooling our lay and clergy leaders to serve in a changing world that is quickly moving away from churches because they are deemed irrelevant.

Questions for Conversation

1. How would you define accountable leadership? What is your experience with accountability inside and outside the United Methodist Church? Compare and contrast these two experiences. Discuss your responses as a group.

2. How does your local congregation hold one another accountable for their discipleship journey, responsibilities of their ministry roles, responsibility to live out the Great Commission, having difficult conversations (i.e., releasing an unpaid ministry worker or confronting a congregational bully), an ineffective pastor or ineffective longtime staff person, etc.? Who takes responsibility, and how are they supported?

3. What type of leadership development have you experienced as a part of the United Methodist Church? How helpful has the church been in equipping you as a spiritual leader to lead your congregation?

4. How would you rate leadership development at your local church for all ages and stages? District? Annual Conference? What brings you to this conclusion? Discuss your ratings with your group.

5. What kind of conversations do you have about the United Methodist Church with unchurched friends, family, neighbors, or co-workers? What is their impression of the United Methodist Church or mainline churches in general? How do you have healthy conversations with them?

6. What do you think we could learn from the franchise model? Does using this model as a metaphor for missional church accountability resonate with you, or do you not see a connection at all? Share your answer with your group and have a discussion.

CHAPTER FIVE
The Cry for Discipling Relationships

In a May 17, 2021, Barna Group ChurchPulse Weekly Podcast, Carey Nieuwhof and Peter Scazzero discussed recent research that shows 74 percent of non practicing Christians would be interested in churches if they had programs and preaching on mental health. One CDC report surveying adults across the United States in late June of 2020 found the following:

- Thirty-one percent of respondents reported symptoms of anxiety or depression
- Thirteen percent reported having started or increased substance use
- Twenty-six percent reported stress-related symptoms
- Eleven percent reported having serious thoughts of suicide in the past 30 days.

These numbers are nearly double the rates we would have expected before the pandemic. There is no doubt that the pandemic affected the mental health of our world, and the degree of that impact is yet to be truly known or understood for years to come.

Interestingly enough, Scazzero "sees the cultivation

of emotional health as a central aspect of the journey of Christian discipleship." He shares, "It's how we understand what it means to be made in God's image as a whole person, in the Hebrew sense of we're whole people, which has different aspects, like relational, social, spiritual, intellectual and emotional. Discipleship has to address all of that."[21]

What better time for the church to be offering community for those seeking community? What better time for the church to be offering relationships for those who are lonely, anxious, and depressed? What better time to be offering Twelve-Step programs? What better time to be offering stress-reduction programs? What better time to be connecting these relational opportunities to the journey of Christian discipleship?

So often, we churches get bogged down in how "we have always done things" that we can't see the forest for the trees. The world is crying out for meaning, relationships, community, and desire to make an impact, but all we can do is offer the same thing we have been doing for the past 20 or 30 years. It is what we have always done and what we are comfortable doing. Anything else would take us outside our comfort zone and make us feel at risk. Are we called to play it safe, or are we called to take risks as disciples and as the church? What can we learn from this parable Jesus taught his disciples in Matthew 25?

---

[21] https://www.barna.com/research/cpw-scazzero-2/

It's also like a man going off on an extended trip. He called his servants together and delegated responsibilities. To one he gave five thousand dollars, to another two thousand, to a third one thousand, depending on their abilities. Then he left. Right off, the first servant went to work and doubled his master's investment. The second did the same. But the man with the single thousand dug a hole and carefully buried his master's money.

After a long absence, the master of those three servants came back and settled up with them. The one given five thousand dollars showed him how he had doubled his investment. His master commended him: "Good work! You did your job well. From now on, be my partner."

The servant with the two thousand showed how he also had doubled his master's investment. His master commended him: "Good work! You did your job well. From now on, be my partner."

The servant given one thousand said, "Master, I know you have high standards and hate careless ways, that you demand the best and make no allowances for error. I was afraid I might disappoint you, so I found a good hiding place and secured your money. Here it is, safe and sound down to the last cent."

The master was furious. "That's a terrible way to live! It's criminal to live cautiously like that! If you knew I was after the best, why did you do less than the least? The least you could have done would have been to invest the sum with the bankers, where at least I would have gotten a little interest.

Take the thousand and give it to the one who risked the most. And get rid of this 'play-it-safe' who won't go out on a limb. Throw him out into utter darkness."

Matthew 25:14-30 (MSG)

115

What's the Great Commission?

A 2019 Barna study on the topic of the Great Commission reported the following:

- Fifty-one percent of churchgoers had not heard of the Great Commission.

- Twenty-five percent had heard of it but were not sure of its meaning.

- Seventeen percent had heard of it and knew the meaning.

When churchgoers were asked if they recognized the Great Commission among other verses:

- Thirty-seven percent accurately chose Matthew 28:18-20.

- Sixteen percent chose the Great Commandment, Matthew 22:37-40.

- Thirty-three percent stated they were not sure if any of the passages were the Great Commission.[22]

Some may think that the study is flawed. Others may think that just because churchgoers don't understand, recognize, or know about the Great Commission doesn't mean they don't know why the church exists. That may be true. Yet, I am troubled by my experience in the vast majority of churches I have worked with over the past

---

[22] https://www.barna.com/research/future-teaching-great-commission/.

decade-plus. At least three or four generations of people in churches have not been fully formed into Christian discipleship.

We have thousands and thousands of members on the books in churches across the country. In most churches, however, only a small fraction of those members are active, and of those active, we have created consumers of programs, not disciples or disciple-makers. It is no wonder churchgoers don't know what the Great Commission is. When members don't know their organization's purpose, it is hard for them to commit to said purpose.

From Members to Disciples to Disciple-Makers

I grew up in a small town in Northwest Missouri with just under four thousand people. While we were too small to have a McDonald's, we did have a Dairy Queen Brazier, and it was *the* premium job to have as a teenager. With two older sisters who worked there before me, it was only fitting that I, too, applied for a job when I turned 16. I got the job and can still make the DQ "curl" when I have access to a self-serve ice cream machine. I share this background to say that I have never worked at McDonald's. I did my fast-food service at the Dairy Queen. But, given the chance, I think I could make the world-renown Big Mac without missing an ingredient. Why is that, you ask? It is not because I am a big fan. In fact, I have never eaten one—I like my burgers with much fewer condiments. But, I could, however, make a Big Mac because of a famous jingle made popular on McDonald's commercials.[23] The tune is so catchy that anytime I start singing it in workshops, most of the room joins in. They remember it. (At least those who are over the age of 40.)

I am sure you are wondering what the relationship of Big Macs is to disciples. Let me connect those dots. Not only did McDonald's train their employees how to make Big Macs, but McDonald's also taught their consumers what was in their Big Macs. And, they did it in such a way that is unforgettable even a couple of decades later.

In contrast, we have parishioners who have been sitting in their pews for years, and sometimes decades, without an idea as to the church's purpose. Worse yet, we have no idea how to make disciples. Think about that. The very purpose for which the church exists – to make disciples – is an unknown recipe for most churches, leaders, and even most pastors. In working with hundreds of churches, it is the minority that has an intentional discipleship pathway. The majority of churches have tried diligently to program their way into attracting new members only to have disappointing results with aging, burned-out volunteers.

In 2019, according to *umdata.org*, the statistics for the United Methodist Church show there were the following:

---

[23] https://www.youtube.com/watch?v=dsuGr4W_QJQ

- 6,487,300 members
- 42,701 professions of faith
- 30,568 congregations
- 2,366,379 in average worship attendance in the U.S.

These numbers mean that there were less than 1.4 average professions of faith per congregation. There was only one profession of faith for every 152 members. There was one profession of faith for every 55.4 attendees. Keep in mind, some churches had many professions of faith while other churches had zero.

The point of this data analysis is, if our organization's purpose is to make disciples who become disciple-makers, we are failing miserably. Imagine how much money a church is spending every year. Think about their return on investment. How much is your church spending for a new profession of faith? Granted, there is hopefully discipling of the already-gathered people going on, too.

Without the ultimate continuous outcome of mature disciples becoming disciple makers and introducing Jesus Christ to new people, how can the church continue without question? What is your church spending to disciple people new in their faith? And, if you were to look at that number over several years, how much has been spent on members instead of disciples becoming disciple-makers?

The bottom line is that Jesus gave us the Great

Commission. Not a great suggestion. We must stop acting like it is a suggestion for disciples and churches. Jesus commanded us. Go! Jesus did not tell us to stay in our pews and wait for people to show up. He said, "Go! Make disciples." Not make members, not programs. He asked us to transform the world, not buildings.

He did not ask us to bury our treasures to keep the lights on until the last funeral was held. No. Jesus commanded us to "Go!" and make DISCIPLES of JESUS CHRIST to TRANSFORM the WORLD!

And this is precisely what our hurting, lonely, depressed, anxious world needs. We just have to connect the dots in meaningful, relevant ways that are not tied to our traditions but are instead highly relational and meaningful to the neighbors we are being called to serve, love, and be in community with.

> *I have a lot more to say about this, but it is hard to get it across to you since you've picked up this bad habit of not listening. By this time you ought to be teachers yourselves, yet here I find you need someone to sit down with you and go over the basics on God again, starting from square one – baby's milk, when you should have been on solid food long ago!*
>
> *Milk is for beginners, inexperienced in God's ways; solid food is for the mature, who have some practice in telling right from wrong.*
>
> **Hebrews 5:11-14 (MSG)**

Being In, Of, and Part of the Community

In my recent book, *Being the Church in the Post-Pandemic World*, I offered what I referred to as eight "game changers" that I believe churches need to make to be vital and healthy in the years to come. Without making these profound, adaptive cultural and leadership changes, churches will struggle to survive. One of these game-changers is being a highly relational church.

There are 15 specific relational shifts churches need to consider:

1. Shift from majority of energy and resources used on the already-gathered faith community to those yet to be gathered

2. Shift from fear or denial of our mission to be in relationship with our neighbors to love, show compassion and empathy for our neighbors

3. Shift from driving into our church on Sunday to being and living as part of the community surrounding the church facility seven days a week

4. Shift from attractional (expecting the community to show up at the building on Sunday) to dispatched movement (disciples sent to share the Good News)

5. Shift from program-driven to more intimate "doing life together" ministries

6. Shift from judgmental to open ears and open hearts

7. Shift from mono-cultural to multicultural and multi-generational

8. Shift from pastor-expected to disciple-responsible relationships

9. Shift from church-centric to community-centric

10. Shift from curriculum-driven to intentional discipleship pathway

11. Shift from self-guided to intentional, relational connections

12. Shift from building-driven to relationally driven for both in-person and virtual ministries

13. Shift from "Sunday perfect" to authentic: raw, real, honest, and vulnerable

14. Shift from top-down to alongside, two-way mentoring and discipling

15. Shift from insular to culturally competent and curious

Of course, in the book, each of these shifts is unpacked to gain some deeper understanding and further clarity, but I hope you can see a common thread weaved throughout this entire list. Yes, that's right. The common thread is becoming a part of the community. A community-centric congregation is a healthy, disciple-making church. We become an inside-out church when we get outside ourselves and see our neighbors as Jesus might see them. We transform ourselves. We become more like Jesus. People are attracted to, and more curious about, people who act more like Jesus than those sitting in a steepled building judging and criticizing – whether we really are or not – others in the community. It is about making ourselves vulnerable. We are likely moving to faith communities that are much less Sunday-centric and building-centric as we move toward much more relationally-centric. Nobody ever said that discipleship was supposed to be comfortable or easy or that it was only for an hour or two on Sundays.

Warm and Friendly Encounters

As we are painfully aware, Generation Z (born between 1997 and 2012) is the most unchurched generation of all time.[24] Some statistics report as low as only 4 percent have a biblical worldview (refers to the framework of ideas and beliefs through which a Christian individual or group interprets the world and interacts with the world). Interestingly enough, recent consultations with members of the Generation Z college population revealed that if one were interested in trying a faith community, the most highly valued thing they would desire is a warm and friendly encounter. Yes, connecting with people in meaningful ways is their top priority. It is not about the music or the venue. It is about how well they are received and how well they connect.

---

[24] https://www.barna.com/research/atheism-doubles-among-generation-z/

Are they greeted warmly and authentically without being overwhelmed? Are they engaged in conversation without being interrogated? Can they see potential new relationships forming with others in the congregation? Do they feel like people in the congregation are authentic and vulnerable? Finding a meaningful community is of the utmost importance to those who would seek a faith community.

The question is, how do we bring others into our faith community? What if we engage with people outside the church walls and within the community in meaningful ways – on their turf first where they feel more comfortable – rather than expecting, hoping, waiting (and perhaps still expecting) them to come to us? We need to become a part of the community where unchurched people hang out. Too often, we churched people spend all of our social time hanging out with mostly other churched people. We need to be intentional about hanging out in places and participating in activities where we will have the opportunity to meet and build new relationships with unchurched people.

Covenant Groups

Becoming disciples is about a continuous next (and deeper) step in our individual faith development. There is no finish line. We will forever be on our life journey in the pursuit of growing more Christ-like. We are continuously reminded that we are better doing this in community with other Jesus followers. We pick each other up along life's way. We share each other's burdens. We keep each other on track. We are encouragers, supporters and ask the difficult questions that fair-weather friends will likely not ask.

Being in a class meeting type of group (small group), often called covenant or life groups today, can play an important role in our discipleship and help guide us in our faith journey. While Sunday school class serves a great purpose to learn, discuss topics of interest, and socialize for an hour each week, a covenant group works to build deeper relationships and journey together toward more meaningful connections.

Typically, a long-term commitment, participants in these smaller groups meet in homes at various times throughout the week and truly experience life together in the deepest sense of the meaning. Group participants know the baggage each carries as well as the baggage that each has set aside. They are raw, vulnerable, and authentic with one another. There is no need to put on the "Sunday facade smile and appearances" for the covenant group. Each can show up and be exactly who they are on any given day at any moment and know they are loved, accepted, and will not be judged in any way. It truly is a come-as-you-are culture. At the same time, the group members also know they will be held accountable for their Christian walk and encouraged to grow and take their next faithful step continually.

It's better to have a partner than go it alone.
Share the work, share the wealth.
And if one falls down, the other helps,
But if there's no one to help, tough!

Two in a bed warm each other.
Alone, you shiver all night.
By yourself you're unprotected.
With a friend you can face the worst.
Can you round up a third?
A three-stranded rope isn't easily snapped.

Ecclesiastes 4:9-12 (MSG)

Coincidently, these are the types of relationships our younger generations hunger for and seek. Granted, they will not tell you they are looking for a "covenant group," but they will share that they are looking for safe places to explore the meaning of life, have conversations about the world in nonjudgmental places with nonjudgmental people, and have spiritual conversations. They want to be able to ask questions and not be told what to believe.

In their beginning stages, these groups might look different than what some of us are used to seeing. Rather than expecting first-time guests to come to us, we need first to reach outwards, start affinity groups, and hang out with unchurched people doing fun activities such as canoeing, gardening, quilting, cooking, golfing, etc. These affinity groups then gradually grow into covenant groups over time. They may or may not ever become a part of the traditional church as we once did, and we need to accept that. Discipleship is not limited, like we sometimes think, inside the church walls. Believe it or not, meaningful discipleship can take place canoeing down a river or playing golf. It is not about how the discipling is happening; it is the fact that discipling is occurring.

Important Reminders

It is important to keep a couple of things in mind. First, in order to grow in individual discipleship, we must understand that it is ultimately our responsibility. We can't blame the church or the pastor for our stunted or delayed growth. As Jesus followers, we are responsible for releasing our dependency on baby's milk and moving on to solid food. We are expected to grow into our faith and ultimately embrace the humbling honor, responsibility and role of disciple-maker. Imagine what kind of energetic movement could occur again if each of us were to embrace the Great Commission as our greatest challenge. If each of us were to disciple just one person each year, we would double in size in a year. In the second year, we could double again. In only five years, this movement could result in 32 times more people knowing Christ. Now, that is a movement!

The second thing we need to keep in mind is that of intentionality. Intentionality, a deliberate, purposeful striving toward growth, is another key component to discipleship. Growing into the likeness of Christ with intentionality and bringing others into the love of Christ is the ongoing pursuit of a disciple's lifetime. This lofty goal may sound intimidating, but the encouraging news is there are numerous pathways, examples, and resources available to help guide us along the way. Check out *Stride* by Schreiner and Willard or *Disciple Like Jesus* by Maynard & Pipkin if you need some resources.

Back to the Basics

Here is where we find ourselves generally as the church around the topic of discipleship. Some have forgotten, and others have never been taught, the purpose of the church. We have fallen victim to what I refer to as the "missional shift." We have shifted away – some, miles and miles away – from our purpose. Some churches have gotten distracted by our selfish, internal focus on taking care of ourselves. Some have become distracted by maintaining the stained-glass windows and the bell towers. And still, others have become distracted by a host of ineffective programs that have caused their members to burn out and sit out. With all the distractions, we have forgotten to focus on the basics of discipleship: the primary focus of discipling new people and the secondary focus of discipling those already gathered. Yes, it is that simple. And, yes, we need to get back to those basics.

All we do, all we have, and all that we schedule must be about discipleship. Period. We will continue to decline until we get discipleship, our mission, the Great Commission, as our primary focus. We have forgotten our purpose! It is time to get back to the basics.

Jesus, undeterred, went right ahead and gave his charge: "God authorized and commanded me to commission you: Go out and train everyone you meet, far and near, in this way of life, marking them by baptism in the threefold name: Father, Son, and Holy Spirit. Then instruct them in the practice of all I have commanded you. I'll be with you as you do this, day after day after day, right up to the end of the age."

Matthew 28:18-20 (MSG)

CHAPTER FIVE
RESPONSE
by Rodney Smothers

We are fortunate to have many resources available to provide solutions to many of the opportunities for developing discipling relationships. In Olu Brown's book, *4D Impact: Smash Barriers Like a Smart Church*, he reminds us that technology, hospitality, worship, and systems are needed to reach current and younger generations.

In their book, *Blank Slate: Write Your Own Rules for a 22nd-Century Church Movement*, Lia McIntosh, Jasmine Rose Smothers, and Rodney Thomas Smothers offer lessons from innovative organizations.

Our current disruptive cultural context – political, social, and theological – makes it difficult to ask others to "follow me to Christ." People have struggled with interpreting laws, systems, and traditions from the beginning days of the New Testament to the present age. Today is no different. There are alternative views of what is right and wrong. Our younger generations ask why they should become a part of the church with judgmental, mean-spirited, and non-accepting messages. Our language does not seem to match our love in practice.

I believe that discipling relationships are possible.

If relationships are the on-ramp to invitational communities, we certainly have to check our bigotry and "isms" at the church door.

In Quincy D. Brown's book, *Discipleship Path: Guiding Congregations to Connect With Jesus*, he begins his discussion with clearing the path, connecting people with Jesus, doing the inward work of discipleship that all of us who are already a part of the church must do. Brown continues his discussion about walking the path through worship, service, growing, giving, impact to completion.

Maybe professions of faith are now the wrong metric. Perhaps encounters for impact are its replacement. The days of people easily joining the church are behind us. Perhaps our challenge is to discern ways to impact people so that they desire to serve, fellowship, and engage in mission and ministry without having to give their lives to an institution. Christ's invitation was not to an institution; it was to a life-changing relationship.

Questions for Conversation

1. What is the greatest relational need in your community? How did you come to this conclusion? How might you have conversations with community leaders to confirm your conclusion?

2. What percentage of your church's ministries are for those already gathered in the church compared to ministries for unchurched people in the community? How might you reverse those percentages?

3. How is your church routinely investing relationally in the community with unchurched people? How are you personally investing routinely and relationally in the community with unchurched people?

4. How many adult professions of faith has your church had in the past five years? How are you celebrating these? How is your church intentional in its pursuit of making new disciples?

5. What is your church's discipleship pathway? How does one go about engaging in the pathway? How are people encouraged to take their next step? How are the church ministries tied to this pathway?

6. How does your church encourage, support, and hold one another accountable for their discipleship journey? Where are you on your faith journey? Who is your discipleship accountability partner?

CHAPTER SIX
The Cry for a Sustainable Strategic Plan for Vitality

People in any organization are always attached to the
obsolete – the things that should have worked but did not,
the things that once were productive and no longer are.

Peter Drucker

While the denomination continues to decline, there seems to be no other plan. Yes, there have been plans to keep the denomination from splitting, and most recently, a plan for splitting amicably. However, there seems to be no turnaround plan or plan for vitality.

Our denomination has spent millions of dollars having conversations around important, emotionally-charged theological differences that have driven wedges between people and congregations. These are indeed important issues. Yet, while we have fought for four decades on one particular subject, the United Methodist Church has continued to decline. And still, we lack a strategic plan, vision, or even really a broadly spoken concern or rally cry from our senior leadership about the decline.

Bureaucracy defends the status quo long past
the time the quo has lost its status.

Laurence J. Peter

Churches, districts, conferences, and general agencies continuously shrink their budgets as their resources dwindle. More often than not, the first line items to be eliminated from budgets are evangelism, community-focused ministries, new church plants, church revitalization, innovations, and leadership development. Positions – and even departments – at district, conference, and agency levels for new church plants, church revitalization, leadership development, innovations, and more are being consolidated or completely eliminated. These practices are like cutting off our noses to spite our faces.

There is no way to recover from the continued decline, let alone start to grow, when an organization takes away most, or all, of the funding for developing new initiatives and new leaders. But repeatedly, this has been and continues to be our practice. Yet, no one seems to be sounding the alarm about this continued self-sabotaging practice.

Let's take a look at Path 1, for example. The creation of Path 1 was affirmed in 2008 as a catalyst to equip 100 church planters and plant 650 new churches by 2012, starting with an $8.5 million General Conference-approved program.[25]

Since its founding in 2008, Path 1 has worked with conferences, districts and local congregations to help create new places for people to connect with God. Path 1 provides training, shares best practices and works to spread

---

[25] http://archives.gcah.org/bitstream/handle/10516/3003/article32.aspx.htm?sequence=3.

innovative ideas across conferences – especially in the United States where denominations across the theological spectrum are seeing declines in attendance.[26]

The intended strategy for Path 1 was for new church starts, and then Path 2 would implement plans for church revitalization. Path 2 has never happened. When Path 1 was created as an organic movement initiated by congregational developers from conferences around the country, these developers felt strongly that Path 1 needed to remain a separate entity not to be swept up in the institution's bureaucracy. This "new plan of action" needed to be nimble, innovative, and not bogged down in the archaic institutionalism driving the unstoppable decline.

Interestingly enough, I was at the table with other congregational developers in the spring of 2019 when it was discovered that Discipleship Ministries (formerly known as the General Board of Discipleship) was in the process of absorbing Path 1 to the point of even considering the elimination of the Path 1 name. It took a group of us congregational developers to intervene and stop this bureaucratic takeover from occurring. In my opinion, it was only partially stopped or maybe only delayed. Path 1 and its budget will likely be gobbled up by the institutional giant slowly and silently enough that no one will notice. What started out as the much-needed innovation has, over time, been eroded and institutionalized.

---

[26] https://www.umnews.org/en/news/growing-impact-of-new-churches

Bureaucracy expands to keep with the needs
of an expanding bureaucracy.

Isaac Asimov

Increasing Complexity and Declining Trust

With each passing General Conference, more and more legislation is added to the *Book of Discipline.* Routinely, when referencing the current *Book of Discipline*, one finds contradictory language because it has been patchworked together since its conception in 1968 when we became the United Methodist Church through the merger of the Evangelical United Brethren Church and the Methodist Church. The original, much smaller *Book of Discipline* dates back to its roots in the 1784 *Book of Discipline* from the Methodist Episcopal Church.

In our book, *Mission Possible: A Simple Structure for Missional Effectiveness,* co-author Blake Bradford and I refer to the traditional structures recommended in the *Book of Discipline* as being perfectly designed to make sure nothing happens. The recommended structures were designed for a culture that no longer exists and for a time that has long passed:

- When institutions were trusted

- When people were calling for stability and constancy

- When serving on an administrative board was one of the few commitments a person had outside their job and home

138

- When life and culture was centered around the church, and the institution's purpose was simply to receive those people into membership

The historic structure is not intended for our non church-centric culture. The structure does not support a time of rapid change nor a culture where quick, sound decisions are needed.

> *Trust always affects two measurable outcomes: speed and cost. When trust goes down – in a relationship, on a team, in a company, in an industry, with a customer – speed decreases with it. Everything takes longer. Simultaneously, costs increase. Redundancy processes, with everyone checking up on everyone else, cost more. In relationships, on teams, in companies, that's a tax. I call it a low-trust tax where literally everything is being taxed off the top. Where trust is low, everything takes longer and costs more.*

Stephen M.R. Covey, *Forbes* [27]

Lack of trust is expensive. When trust is lacking, processes and decisions move slower. More checks and balances are required. People are more suspicious and cautious. More questions are asked. All these extra steps slow down any processes in the system and the resulting decisions. Because of the lack of trust, those tasked with making decisions are more cautious and deliberate in making decisions knowing that every decision will likely be questioned and scrutinized. All of these extra steps and time delays are costly to the institution. They cost actual dollars, loss of productivity, higher employee turnover, and lower morale.

---

[27] https://www.forbes.com/sites/rodgerdeanduncan/2018/07/12/the-speed-of-trust-its-a-learnable-skill/?sh=10796f243bbf

CRY FROM THE PEW

These are just some of the reasons our younger generations find it frustrating to serve in our structures and often don't find the structures to be effective or efficient. They see them as a waste of time and will likely not serve in these ineffective, redundant, and outdated structures. And while the multiple committees are supposed to create a system of checks and balances, our leaders have a strong reluctance to hold one another accountable. It is this complexity, added to the lack of accountability, that has led to the lack of trust. We no longer live in a join-and-submit type of culture. Add a lack of transparency, a heavy-handed, top-down approach, and you have yourself a recipe for a disastrous institutional decline leading to extinction.

> *Any intelligent fool can make things bigger and more complex. It takes a touch of genius and a lot of courage to move in the opposite direction.*
>
> **Albert Einstein**

Casting Vision

> *When there's no vision, the people get out of control but whoever obeys instruction is happy.*
>
> **Proverbs 29:18 (CEB)**

> *Where there is no revelation, people cast off restraint; but blessed is the one who heeds wisdom's instruction.*
>
> **Proverbs 29:18 (NIV)**

Where there is no vision, the people perish:
but he that keepeth the law, happy is he.

Proverbs 29:18 (KJV)

If people can't see what God is doing,
they stumble all over themselves;
But when they attend to what he reveals,
they are most blessed.

Proverbs 29:18 (MSG)

Creating pathways for survival is not the same as casting vision. Vision is what creates a new life cycle in an organization. Vision helps create energy, motivation, momentum, excitement and alignment. It legitimizes leadership, motivates more profound generosity, and provides a deeper sense of community and collaboration.

While we have driven home our purpose (our mission) as a denomination over the past decade or so, has our senior leadership provided a compelling vision for the future? Has there been a discernment for what God's preferred future is for Methodism? While I understand there has been deep conversation around particular theological topics of concern – and rightly so – there seems to be no conversation or purposeful vision-casting for where we as Methodists are headed or where God is calling us.

The most pathetic person in the world is someone
who has sight, but has no vision.

Helen Keller

I find the various translations of Proverbs 29:18 about vision fascinating. While some translations cite

141

"vision," other translations refer to "revelations" or "see what God is doing." When it talks about a lack of vision, one translation cites "the people will perish," and other translations state "the people cast off restraints," "stumble all over themselves," or "get out of control." And lastly, the translations of the same verse span from being happy by keeping the law and obeying God's instruction to being blessed by heeding what God reveals. In other words, without vision, revelations, or paying attention to what God is doing, we will perish, cast off restraints, stumble all over ourselves, or get out of control. But when we obey God/the law, attend to what God reveals, or heed God's wisdom, we will be (most) blessed or happy.

As an eternal optimist and taking some liberties as a published author for over 14 years, I translate it like this: If God's people can't see what God is revealing, they are destined to live an unhappy, self-absorbed life full of emptiness. But, for those who faithfully pursue what God reveals to them, they will be blessed beyond what they can imagine, and God will be able to use them and their God-given gifts to build the Kingdom.

In his book *Visioneering*, Andy Stanley paints a compelling argument regarding the need for visioning:

> *What is a vision? Where do they come from? Visions are born in the soul of a man or woman who is consumed with the tension between what is and what could be. Anyone who is emotionally involved – frustrated, brokenhearted, maybe even angry – about the way things are, in light of the way they believe things could be, is a candidate for a*

vision. Visions form in the hearts of those who are dissatisfied with the status quo. Vision carries with it a sense of conviction. Anyone with a vision will tell you this is not merely something that could be done. This is something that should be done.

So, where is our sense of conviction? Where is our tension of what is and what could be/should be? What do we feel must absolutely be done? Are we not yet frustrated or brokenhearted enough to be convicted that something must be done?

> *A vision is not just a picture of what could be;*
> *it is an appeal to our better selves,*
> *a call to become something more.*
>
> **Rosabeth Moss Kanter**

I also love this quote by Tom Bandy found in the foreword of *Winning on Purpose* by John Edmund Kaiser. While it speaks to mission accountability, I believe it also speaks to vision as the two are so closely tied together:

> *Are you prepared to stake everything,*
> *change anything,*
> *and do whatever it take*
> *even if it means altering long-familiar habits,*
> *redeveloping precious programs*
> *and redeploying sacred assets?*

Isn't that ultimate accountability for the mission of making disciples: when we are called to a unique vision, when we are willing to let go of all that is familiar, be uncomfortable for the sake of where God is calling us into a new future, and we do whatever it takes? Now, that is something that I believe people will get behind and become excited about.

Are we spending time discerning God's preferred future for our beloved church? Or are we simply spinning our wheels, using our resources trying to figure out how to maintain or sustain a dying institution? Are we being faithful to God using God's resources in this way? What is the denominational ROI (return on investment) since 1968? Think of all the energy, time, dollars, and emotional turmoil expended in the past five decades-plus. While good things have happened along the way, have we really done all we could do? Or have we wasted too many precious resources on institutional bureaucracy? How can we do better as we move forward?

Who is responsible for casting such vision? Our episcopal leadership? The Connectional Table? Does it need to be another called group? I often wonder if the bureaucratic layers are so thick and convoluted that no one really knows or can discern if they have the authority to make necessary changes. Furthermore, does any such group trust that the greater membership would buy into such a vision at this point? Or do we just need to start over with something new and much simpler?

Psychological Safety

Drawing on the extensive research done by Harvard

Business School Professor Amy C. Edmundson, *psychological safety* is the belief that one will not be punished or humiliated for speaking up with ideas, questions, concerns, or mistakes. When psychological safety is present on a team, it facilitates organizational learning, innovation, and meaningfulness via the willing contribution of ideas and actions to a shared purpose.[28]

How much psychological safety is present in our church culture? At the general church level? Conference level? District? Local church?

Obviously, it will vary from place to place. Still, overall, I am not sure that we have been intentional, let alone successful, about creating a culture that promotes and nurtures psychological safety. In fact, it is quite the opposite in many environments, and one is discouraged from asking questions, coming up with suggestions, or dreaming of new innovative ideas.

> *In a psychologically unsafe workplace,*
> *you hear a lot of good news.*
> *If you're hearing too much happy talk,*
> *it's probably an indication you're not hearing*
> *enough of the straight talk.*
> *Psychological safety is a belief that the context*
> *is safe for interpersonal risks.*
>
> **Amy Edmondson**[29]

---

[28] https://www.forbes.com/sites/paulspiegelman/2021/06/06/psychological-safety-takes-years-to-develop-and-seconds-to-shatter/?sh=4f8d1380158c.

[29] https://careynieuwhof.com/episode430/.

Whatever lies ahead for us must include a nurturing culture of psychological safety. Without it, we cannot build a culture of creativity, cultural relevance, innovation, spiritually mature and vulnerable disciple-making disciples, or a faithful, sustainable pathway forward.

Tweaks or Organic Innovation: A Call to Action

If I only had an hour to chop down a tree,
I would spend the first 45 minutes sharpening my axe.

Abraham Lincoln

We all know the definition of *insanity*, right? It is doing the same thing over and over, but expecting a different outcome. As we find ourselves waiting for a delayed 2020 General Conference possibly to occur in late 2022, I wonder if we are really ready for innovation or are we just going to kick the proverbial can down the road once again. While some say they won't wait until 2024 to leave the church, I wonder if progress can be made. The process is so cumbersome, time- consuming, and so many people are involved. And frankly, in today's world, four years is an eternity to wait for things to change – not to mention the additional time added because of the pandemic.

Maybe some forward progress will be made. Perhaps people will begin to make decisions regardless of what happens at General Conference. The Global Methodist Church (GMC) has done a great job of laying the groundwork with a *Transitional Book of Doctrines and Discipline* as well as a *Judicial Practice and Procedure Rules* and has named a Transitional Leadership Council. Other potential new expressions of Methodism have been named but have not made anywhere close to the GMC's progress in laying the groundwork.

What happens to those remaining in the United Methodist Church if there is an agreement made to separate into multiple "tracks" of Methodism? What happens to individuals whose church decides to go one direction and they desire to go another? From my understanding, no one is working to simplify, improve, or solve the complexity and issues in the current *Book of Discipline's* issues. Man, certainly not all, are identified in this book. I have heard some say that those remaining will just simply pass legislation to "clean up" the *Book of Discipline.* Are you kidding me? That will take the rest of our lifetimes. We don't have that much time. Frankly, that simply makes no sense. Start from scratch. It will be far cleaner, less time-consuming, and should be a reduction rather than an addition of pages, structure, rules, bureaucracy, layers, labels, and institutionalism. What are we waiting for? We need to be working on this *now*!

"Don't be afraid to take big steps when one is indicated. You can't cross a chasm in two small jumps."

David Lloyd George (1863-1945), Politician

147

Let's not stop there. Maybe what is needed is not just a new *Book of Discipline*. Maybe the whole institution needs to be re-thought, re-built, or torn down and innovated with a whole new model. Again, I'm not convinced that Wesley ever intended Methodists to be an institution. What could honor our roots, address the cultural distrust of institutions, empower laity once again, break down the hierarchy, remove the expensive and expansive bureaucratic layers, and create an organic movement that is relevant and less real-estate dependent? Why aren't we having conversations about this type of innovation rather than preservation of the institution?

Why aren't we inviting both laity and clergy, both older and younger generations, to the table with a blank slate of what is possible? Why aren't neutral people – not agency executives, bishops, employees, lobbying/ special interest groups, special interests – included at the table? Let's rethink leadership. Let's rethink polity. Let's rethink structure. Let's rethink shared resources and backroom operations and inefficient systems with efficiency and options for local contextualization so churches can move forward and operate with a cohesive vision and mission. Let's build in accountability with transparency. Let's make a commitment to on-going innovation and leadership development. Let's create a vital and strategic plan that is sustainable rather than starting off with a failing institutional framework.

Modern society is built upon two things: truth, which is discovered, and innovation, which is created.

True Tamplin, Founder of Finance Strategists

It feels like we are on the precipice of enormous possibilities, but instead we are wasting it by sitting on our hands. It is as though we realize we are on the sinking *Titanic* and have already taken on considerable water. All the life rafts have been deployed. Yet, those still on the ship are trying to use duct tape to seal the gaping hole in the hull.

The riskiest thing we can do is just maintain the status quo.

Bob Iger, Media Executive & Businessman

Friends, let's step out in faith! God is trying to use us to do a new thing! Maybe we are the ones that God is trying to use for such a time as this! Are we going to sit in our "palaces" and drink our wine? Or are we going to roll up our sleeves and get to work? Let's be bold and courageous. Let's take a much more dramatic, innovative approach to what could be a much brighter, and more optimistic future and create something far greater than anything we could ever imagine so our children, grandchildren, and great-great-grandchildren might have a relationship with Jesus.

This is what God says,

the God who builds a road right through the ocean,

who carves a path through pounding waves,

The God who summons horses and chariots and armies –

they lie down and then can't get up;

they're snuffed out like so many candles:

"Forget about what's happened;

don't keep going over old history.

Be alert, be present. I'm about to do something brand-new.

It's bursting out! Don't you see it?

There it is!"

Isaiah 43:16-19 (MSG)

CHAPTER SIX
RESPONSE
by Rodney Smothers

This chapter and Kay's discussion regarding Path 1 hit me particularly hard because, like Kay, I was deeply involved in Path 1 and believed, with my whole heart, it was a legitimate pathway to making disciples of Jesus Christ. As a conference developer and proponent of its strategy and promise, I, too, grieved when it got sidelined by other denominational priorities.

I have seen many strategic plans both at denominational levels and annual conference levels come and go because of a change in leadership, a shifting of priorities, or a lack of a commitment to invest beyond one quadrennium of funding. But help is on the way.

Technology, social media, podcasts, webinars, virtual training, and on-line platforms provide us with an abundance of ways to acquire the tools we need to progress in making disciples of Jesus Christ. Unfortunately, we are distracted by a health pandemic and a denominational pandemic that both are draining resources away from our strategic focus.

In some cases, our denominational leaders are distracted, just trying to keep their conferences vital.

In the other cases, people are waiting for the coming denominational split. And unfortunately, there is a group of people who really don't care, as long as there is enough money left to fund their retirement accounts.

And then there are people like Kay and me and some of you who pray, coach, teach, workshop, seminar, and facilitate to equip and encourage a generation of learners and leaders, lay and clergy, who are willing to pursue God's vision for vital church ministry. Maybe I am just old- school and believe that the old gospel hymn leads the way when we sing, "God never fails, God never fails, God abides in me, gives me victory, God never fails. Just keep the faith and never cease to pray, walk upright, Call God day noon or night. God will be there, there's no need to worry, for God never fails."

Our call to action is to equip and mature spiritual leaders who can disciple others to keep their hearts and mind on the main thing: leading others into a relationship with Jesus Christ through witness, worship, and invitation.

Questions for Conversation

1. What dreams do you have for a future faith community for generations to come?

2. What sacrifices are you willing to make today so that more persons from the future generations will have a relationship with Jesus?

3. What bold, courageous steps do you believe the United Methodist Church is being called to take to be a vital, healthy, disciple-making movement for generations to come? How will you personally be a part of it? What's the first step?

4. It is no accident that you are reading this resource at this very moment. Something is stirring inside you. How is God calling you "for such a time as this?

5. As Tom Bandy asks, "Are you prepared to stake everything, change anything, and do whatever it takes – even if it means altering long familiar habits, redeveloping precious programs, and redeploying sacred assets" to be bold, courageous, and innovative to reach new people? Who will you invite to come alongside you?

6. What is essential to take with you on the new journey, and what can be shed and left behind? Share your insights and thought-processes with your group.

Your Call to Action

Without action, our cries will go unanswered. Conversations are a start, but action will ultimately get us to our desired destination. What specifically is your call to action? Following is a recap of the topics, suggestions, and possible next steps for your consideration. Take a look at the list. Spend some time in prayer and discernment as to where God is calling you into action. Maybe it is at the local church level. Maybe it is at your district or conference level. Maybe God is calling you to lead a call to action at the Jurisdictional or General Conference level.

Record your call to action below. Wherever it is that God is calling you, be assured that God has already laid the path before you. Be bold and courageous for such a time as this!

Summary of Potential Call to Action Steps

- Gather a small group in your local congregation to study this resource together and decide your individual or group call to action.

- Gather with other leaders in your district to study this resource together and decide your individual or group call to action together.

- Contact your elected conference delegation for conversation about where you are feeling a call to action.

- Consider writing legislation for a general conference.

- If you are an elected delegate, consider gathering your delegation together to study this resource together. Consider hosting other delegations, too, to enrich the conversation. What is your collective call to action?

- Knowing new movements start at the fringes, consider where there is energy at the fringes that could be tapped into for an innovative call to action.

- Who are influential innovators that have leverage and voice that would collaborate with you or your group in your bold call to action?

- How might you (or your small group) think not just outside the box, but as though there was no box at all when considering what your call to action might look like?

- If you were to create a faith community "network" for the post-modern world of tomorrow, how would you organize it? Who would you need to collaborate with to make sure you thought through all the different angles necessary to ensure you have a simplistic yet comprehensive approach? Who would you want to pitch this to so it could become a reality?

- What is the bare minimum you believe must be done at the next general conference? If you had a magic wand and could fix all that was broken, what all would you change. repair, create, or eliminate at the next general conference? Create a list of both scenarios, gather a group for discussion, and share why each suggestion is needed. Hear their input and suggestions. What is the resulting call to action you are sensing?

My Call to Action

_____

_____

_____

_____

_____

_____

_____

_____

Afterword

From Kay

For those of you who know me, these writings are likely not surprising – perhaps a bit bolder than I would typically share in writing or in a public setting but not surprising. For those of you experiencing me for the first time, I am sure some of what I have shared is quite shocking, and even more so knowing it is coming from a layperson. If I have offended anyone personally, please know that was not at all my intent. As shared in the introduction, I created this resource from a sense of calling and, as an apostle and prophet, to hold up the mirror and create a space with a sense of urgency for much-needed – and seemingly avoided – conversation.

I hope that conversations will ensue, resulting in a catalyst for innovation, creativity, and adaptive leadership that will birth something more beautiful than we can ever imagine as a new, simple, unencumbered, disciple-making movement that reaches millions of people. Lord, let it be so.

Hear our cry. Oh Lord, hear the cry of your church!

From Rodney

The interesting thing about co-authoring a book is that the readers have the benefit of experiencing the thoughts of the authors when they intersect and when they travel in dramatically different directions. Kay and I are both passionate about transformation, next-level leadership, and the development of healthy, vital systems.

My more extensive thoughts are spelled out in detail in the book *Resurgence: Navigating the Changing Ministry Landscape*, which I co-authored with Rev. Dr. Candace M. Lewis, the president-dean of Gammon Theological Seminary. In the final chapter of that book, Dr. Lewis and I stated that leadership is the most crucial ingredient in congregational resurgence.

We did not stop there, however. We also stated that churches must reprioritize the significance of spiritual formation for laity and clergy. Ephesians 4:11-16, reminds us that our primary role is to equip God's people for works of service. I have served in pastoral ministry for forty years. As I think about the future, the one thing that sustains me every day, is the instructions of the men and women, lay and clergy, who encouraged me to keep pressing on.

In this book, we have not solved all the church's problems, but What we have attempted to productively engage others in conversation about our beloved church's future, not its demise.